Oldest San Francisco

A Guide to Historic Treasures

Alec Scott

Reedy Press

Reedy Press
PO Box 5131
St. Louis, MO 63139
www.reedypress.com

Library of Congress Control Number: 2023938887

ISBN: 9781681064994

Cover Design: Jill Halpin
Book Design: Linda Eckels

Photos courtesy of the author unless otherwise noted.

Cover photo credit, clockwise from top left: Alec Scott, Center Hardware, Boudin Bakery, Alec Scott. Author headshot by Katherine Emery.

Printed in the United States of America
23 24 25 26 27 5 4 3 2 1

Table of Contents

ACKNOWLEDGMENTS

My husband David Bruckmann has helped in the research—and joined in the adventures—that went into this book. Thank you for your love and support.

My thanks to Kerstin Stanley Clark who introduced me to San Francisco. And to William Scott, who taught here, came through the fire here—and who helped me keep that feeling for San Francisco alive. And to Lisa Morehouse, Emily Wilson, and James Bullard, who made us feel at home after we moved here.

My friend and former colleague Eileen Whitfield contributed invaluable editorial advice. The author of *Secret San Francisco*, Ruth Carlson, was a help and resource throughout. My longtime editor at the *San Francisco Chronicle*, Deb Wandell, commissioned some of the pieces that helped me get up to speed on my adopted city. My thanks also to Josh Stevens, Barbara Northcott, Morgan Hoffman, and the team at Reedy Press.

I relied on many distinguished San Franciscans—too many to name—to help in the research of the book's entries.

Thank you, all of you, for taking the time to speak to me. Any errors and omissions are mine—not yours!

Introduction

I fell for San Francisco right away. I came here to visit a college friend in a place on Telegraph Hill, looking out over Alcatraz. When my friend was called away, I was left on my own with a powder-blue Volkswagen Bug at my disposal. Its brakes weren't the best, and I was driving up and down some hilly streets. But the chance to get to know this city on my own was great.

I began with a visit to the Japanese Tea Garden—the oldest such public garden in the country—in Golden Gate Park. I had dim sum in the continent's oldest Chinatown. I bought some books by the Beat Generation at City Lights, the nation's first paperback bookstore, and read them at Caffe Trieste, the city's first espresso house. I went to Haight-Ashbury to look for traces of the counterculture and found that the free clinic that cared for the flower children was still open. And, as a young, straight-laced kid from small-town Ontario, I ventured to the Castro, where I was inspired by its massive rainbow flag waving in the breeze to acknowledge that, though I was straight-laced, I wasn't straight.

These things are still here—the flag waves, espressos are still being pulled at Caffe Trieste—and they feature in these pages. What follows are some of the institutions that helped make San Francisco what it is: an entrepreneurial, future-oriented city with a strong sense of its past.

—Alec Scott, 2023

Downtown

EMBARCADERO, FINANCIAL DISTRICT, UNION SQUARE
CHINATOWN, NOB HILL

1898

OLDEST CIVIC CLOCK TOWER

FERRY BUILDING

1 Embarcadero

The Ferry Building boasts the oldest clock tower on a civic building in town, one of the oldest in the nation, and it is the oldest ferry terminal in the city. The building was born under a shadow. Its young designer, A. Page Brown, had trained with the most famous firm in the country, New York's McKim, Mead & White, which designed public buildings that riffed on classical and renaissance motifs. Brown's tower was based on the Giralda bell tower on the cathedral in Seville, Spain. But after he finalized the designs, he was thrown from a horse and died.

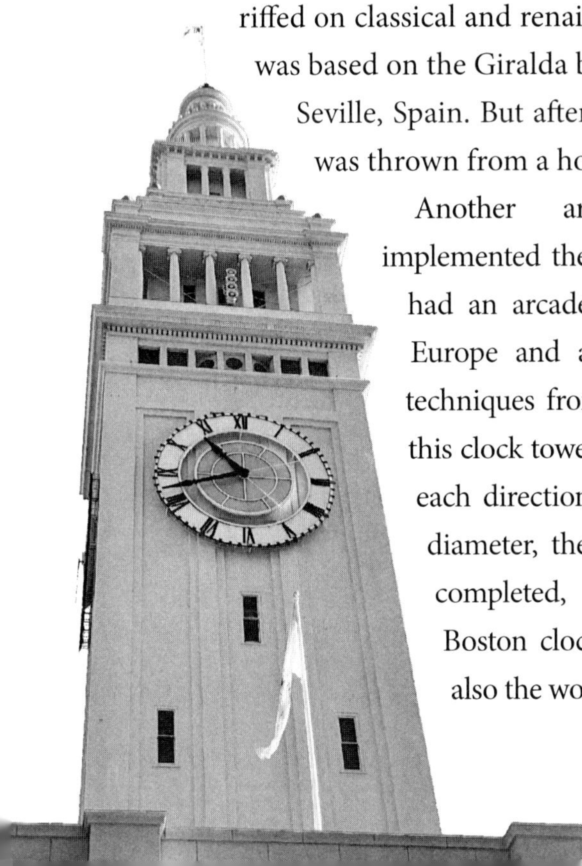

Another architect, Howard Swain, implemented the plans. The finished building had an arcade like certain monasteries in Europe and a mosaic floor created with techniques from ancient Rome. And it had this clock tower, with four clocks, one facing each direction. Their faces were 22 feet in diameter, the largest in the world. When completed, the whole thing, done by Boston clockmaker E. Howard Co., was also the world's largest wind-up clock.

The Ferry Building cheated death soon after its completion. The 1906 quake occurred at 5:16 a.m. The time was frozen on the clocks, but their heavy mechanism didn't tumble down the tower. Though the building trembled, it did not fall. And the man supervising the city's response to the disaster, Gen. Frederick Funston, ordered the navy and harbor's fireboats to pump saltwater over it, saving it from the blaze.

By the 1930s the Ferry Building had become the second-busiest transit hub in the world, bested only by London's Charing Cross Station. For a time it was also the center of one of the busiest ports in the world. But in the 1930s, when the magnificent Bay and Golden Gate Bridges went up and Oakland came into its own as a port, ferry and ship traffic rapidly diminished. In 1958 the last ferry sailed, and soon enough the Harbor Commission proposed getting rid of the building in favor of a 40-story San Francisco World Trade Center. But interest faded in the project, and the building languished, its mosaics covered in linoleum by new tenants, its view from Market Street obscured by the construction of the elevated Embarcadero Expressway.

But it just had to wait things out a bit. In 1989, the Loma Prieta earthquake took down the expressway. Some ferry traffic returned to the bay, and, in food-mad San Francisco, the Ferry Building became the chief temple to all things edible. In 1992 a farmers' market proved such a success that it became a ritual three times a week. In 2003, after a restoration of the terminal—one that involved removing the linoleum from the mosaics—food businesses and restaurants of all sorts were added to the ground floor. Among them, over the years, were a chocolatier, a mushroom company, a bakery, and an oyster bar.

Newspaper columnist Herb Caen described his deep fondness for the Ferry Building. Those who don't live here, he wrote, "have never seen the far-off windows of the East Bay, touched with fire for an instant by the dying sun . . . They've never listened to the thick hush of a clear dawn over the Bay, when the waters are still asleep and even the Ferry Building seems to have its tower tucked under a wing."

Though the Ferry Building's is among the only historic clock towers in San Francisco, it is not alone. The elevated freeway that goes south from the Bay Bridge makes a swooping curve around a clock tower built in 1921, attached to the Max Schmidt Lithography Company building (461 2nd St.). In the 1990s, architect David Baker converted the 230,000-square-foot structure into one of the city's first live-work buildings, with a penthouse incorporating the tower.

Another old public clock is much smaller. Put up in 1915, the Albert Samuels Clock (856 Market St.) is the city's oldest extant street clock. If you peer into it, you can see the word "Lucky" inscribed inside. Some say this is a tiny memorial to Elias "Lucky" Baldwin, who once built a hotel nearby. Married four times, he made and lost at least two fortunes. Once larger than life, he is now remembered, in part, because of one word in a clock.

1903

Oldest Public-Affairs Forum

Commonwealth Club

110 Embarcadero

"In a nation as polarized as ours now is, the club's mission, to foster respectful public dialogue about important subjects, is as vital as it's ever been." These words are from Gloria Duffy, the longtime president of the Commonwealth Club, the nation's oldest and largest public-affairs forum. Her leadership has helped freshen up the group's once-stodgy image.

For many years, the club seemed a place where, after three bangs of the gavel and much throat-clearing, a procession of Old Boys, some distinguished, some not, aired their views. That said, the distinguished among these gents were very distinguished indeed, with both Presidents Roosevelt, Teddy and Franklin Delano, addressing the group, along with the likes of Martin Luther King Jr., Dwight Eisenhower, and Nikita Khrushchev.

If the settings leaned toward the plush and cozy—some early meetings were held in a grand ballroom at the St. Francis Hotel—the subjects discussed were down to earth, even gritty. Early studies focused on child labor (1906), aboriginal rights (1909), and air pollution (1913). Some discussions led to reformist legislation, including acts on the selection of jurors, the appointment of public defenders, and banking. In 1924, just four years after the first commercial radio broadcast, the club put more in this vein on the

airwaves with a public-affairs program that is still going—making it the host of the oldest radio show in the country.

Perhaps the biggest bombshell speech of the club's early years was the younger Roosevelt's talk in 1932, in which he sketched the outlines of legislation that would come to be known as the New Deal. Vice President Dan Quayle made another news-making speech in 1992, a critique of sit-com character Murphy Brown, a television anchorwoman played by Candice Bergen. In an early salvo in the culture wars, he blamed her for "mocking the importance of fathers, by bearing a child—alone."

By then, women members were in the audience, as they'd been allowed to join in 1971. One of the first female members, former child star and diplomat Shirley Temple Black, later became club president. Under Black and later Duffy, the mix of speakers began to shift, with primatologist Jane Goodall, local congresswoman Nancy Pelosi, and Black Lives Matter cofounder Alicia Garza taking to its podium.

"When I came on board, things needed some shaking up," says Duffy. She's a nuclear arms expert who worked high-up in the Department of Defense under Bill Clinton and once roomed with Condoleezza Rice. On her watch the club went digital. It now has more than 18 million views on its YouTube channel. And after years of moving its proceedings from one venue to the next, the group finally built a $33-million headquarters on the waterfront. The handsome, glass-fronted building with multiple auditoriums is state-of-the-art and media-wise, has a great rooftop deck and garden, and is environmentally friendly enough to earn a LEED Gold certification.

The subjects, as always, range from hard-hitting to policy-wonkish, with recent topics including homelessness, climate change, water scarcity, violence against Asian Americans, and the role of propositions in California's governance. When Ayaan Hirsi Ali spoke of women's rights in the Muslim world, her talk sparked controversy, in-house and out. "We were asked to cancel her speech," Duffy says. "We went ahead with it in the interests of free speech."

She says this decision led the organization to look at "free speech and its boundaries . . . [to look] at hate speech. We're open to different views, but not ones based on false narratives. Still, the basic idea remains the same, people make better, more informed decisions after such discussions. There needs to be a public square."

In the 1930s, the International Longshoremens' Association, a union, had offices here. Failing in its push for increased pay and reduced hours, the ILA ordered its workers to stop unloading ships in 1934. When police escorted cargo from the piers, they met with opposition from the strikers. The police then raided a union mess hall, shooting three and killing two, on what came to be called Bloody Thursday After the killings, the union's leader, Harry Bridges, organized a funeral procession through the streets of San Francisco and labor leaders joined in, calling for a general strike to shut down the city for four days.

Congress later enacted labor legislation that led to long-sought pay hikes and shorter work weeks.

1854

Oldest Cathedral

OLD ST. MARY'S

660 California St.

This first cathedral on the West Coast has been waging war on sin for the better part of two centuries. The message on the bell tower is given extra emphasis with capital letters: "SON, OBSERVE THE TIME AND FLY FROM EVIL." Inside, a painting above the altar shows an angel crushing a devil underfoot—underlining the Church's core message over time.

But, as often as not, the bell tower's warning to fly from evil fell on deaf ears, with the brothels of the Barbary Coast nearby. These houses of ill repute often employed barkers on the street, though, according to historian Herbert Asbury, "some of the women did their own ballyhooing, leaning from a window." Fed up, a St. Mary's priest collaborated with the Society of the Prevention of Vice in a crusade against the brothels in the late 1800s.

One of San Francisco's archbishops harrumphed, "The location of the . . . Cathedral is such that it can scarcely be approached from any direction without a shudder at the sinfulness and filth of its surroundings." So, the diocese set about building a replacement, also named St. Mary's, at Van Ness and O'Farrell. When it was completed in 1891, there was some talk of taking down the old one, but an American order of priests, the Paulists, got approval to carry on in the building that is now, of course, known as Old St. Mary's. (The New St. Mary's got its own comeuppance when another, even newer St. Mary's, an architecturally adventurous cathedral, was built to replace it in 1970.)

Though Old St. Mary's survived the quake in 1906, the ensuing fire destroyed much of its innards. A Paulist father, fleeing up Nob Hill, shot the surreal (and much circulated) image of flames engulfing the walls and tower. There was talk of not rebuilding, or of starting from scratch, but as local architect Willis Polk said, "To tear down the standing walls of Old St. Mary's is to tear down history itself." And so, using some of the old materials and following much of the old design, the church rose again, reopening in 1909.

Another era, another peril: Old St. Mary's was shaken, but not badly damaged, in the 1989 Loma Prieta quake. Still, it struggled for years afterward to fund the retrofits needed to meet new safety regulations. A window still in need of particular care is one that features the order's patron saint, Paul, on the road to Damascus.

Still, even with peeling paint and a staff of five, the church limps on, trying to meet its mandate to minister to the neighborhoods that have grown up around it, the financial district and Chinatown. There, the church was long known as "Dai Chung Low"—big bell building, according to historian Philip P. Choy. The cathedral has often hosted free classical concerts at lunchtime, popular with the traders working in nearby skyscrapers, and some of its masses and its on-site nursery school are conducted in both English and Cantonese.

Suitably, materials used in Old St. Mary's reflect its connection to East and West: the granite came from China, the bricks from New England. But the beams supporting the roof are all California, made from local redwood.

Today, right across California Street, where a few of the Barbary Coast's more notorious brothels once operated, there is a park with a memorial to 97 Chinese-Americans who fought on behalf of the US in WWI and WWII. One senses that that the founders of Old St. Mary's would approve.

Across Grant Ave. are two buildings that speak to the long, often difficult road that Chinese Americans have had to establish themselves here. After the post-quake fire leveled this area, there was a proposal to move Chinatown to the city's southern fringes, a neighborhood of mud flats now known as Hunters Point. The local community's leaders fought this proposal, in part by swiftly rebuilding, getting two art and antiquities bazaars (the Sing Fat Company and the Sing Chong Building) up within two years. These were the first buildings in Chinatown to incorporate Asian architectural motifs—pagoda-like canopies on the rooftops, curly-tipped eaves, a dragon carved on one, a trigram on the other. Eventually, Look Tin Eli, the manager of Sing Chong, cofounded the Canton Bank, the first bank run by Chinese Americans. In time, both art bazaars went out of business, but the buildings still speak eloquently of Chinatown's refusal to be moved.

1835

OLDEST PUBLIC PLAZA

PORTSMOUTH SQUARE

San Francisco's first city planner was a Swiss grocer and tavern keeper named Jean-Jacques Vioget, whose qualification for his city planner role may have been his possession of surveying tools. He set Portsmith Square aside for public gatherings during the period when California belonged to Mexico, naming it the Plaza de Yerba Buena—Yerba Buena being the name of what was then a sleepy small town.

In the late 1840s the Plaza got two rude awakenings. The first came when US Navy Commodore John Montgomery sailed into the bay in the USS *Portsmouth* and officially claimed the region on behalf of the United States. The ship eventually gave the square its current name. The second came when Mormon newspaper editor Sam Brannan rushed into the plaza carrying a quinine bottle full of gold dust, yelling, "Gold! Gold! Gold from the American River!"

This has been called the shout heard 'round the world, and it brought thousands here to join the Gold Rush. Flush with money and people, the square was soon lined with bars and gambling houses. At the El Dorado bar, bartender Jerry Thomas prepared his signature Blue Blazer for a crowd of gamblers, drinkers, and call girls, while outside the occasional itinerant preacher held forth about the perils of vice. The square also witnessed at least one hanging, that of an Australian named John Jenkins. Reports had Jenkins chewing tobacco calmly as he met his end. In addition, a posse assembled in the square to go after the Sydney Ducks, a gang led by Australians who'd been terrorizing the city by periodically lighting it on fire.

Portsmouth Square witnessed other, less violent firsts. The state's first public schoolhouse stood on it, dating from 1848. In 1851 the first baseball games were played here, and in 1873 the first cable car ran up Clay, one of the streets lining the square. The city's first theatrical performance, a double bill of *The Wife* and *Charles the Second*, was staged at a makeshift theatre here.

Late in the 1870s writer Robert Louis Stevenson arrived in San Francisco following a married woman he'd fallen for at an artists' retreat in France. He lived on Bush Street and is supposed to have sunned himself often in the square while he waited for her to extricate herself from her marriage. After his death in 1894, a monument to him went up in the square. It was a bronze galleon, modeled on the one sailed by Long John Silver in *Treasure Island*. But if Stevenson's legacy is well marked, the stories and names of those buried in the square in haste after the 1906 quake are mainly lost.

As the years passed, San Francisco's Chinatown grew to encompass the area. On the square proper is a statue of a woman with a torch, modeled on the Goddess of Democracy built by protesters on Tiananmen Square in 1989. But there are those in San Francisco's Chinatown who recognize the communist government as legitimate, and they gathered here in 1979, when the US, under President Richard Nixon, reestablished diplomatic ties with China. Their nationalist rivals responded with a rally near Washington Square.

Portland Square's look has changed over the years—of course it has. In 1971 a pedestrian bridge went up over Kearny Street, connecting the square with a Chinese Cultural Center and the Hilton Hotel. At present, there are plans to demolish this underused "Bridge to Nowhere" as part of a $66-million renovation of the square, a once-dusty plaza that woke up in the mid-19th century, and has been wide awake ever since.

The city's oldest Chinese restaurant, Sam Wo (713-715 Clay St.), recently relocated to the square. Founded shortly after the 1906 quake, it became known as a low-cost, late-night joint, serving rice-noodle rolls and jook to generations. In the 1950s the cash-strapped Beat writers came here; later, tourists came as well, hoping to get insulted by Edsel Ford Fung, dubbed the rudest waiter in the world. A sign in the joint read: No Booze, No Jive, No Coffee, No Milk, Soft Drinks, Fortune Cookies.

When Sam Wo was shut down by authorities for health and safety reasons in 2012, there were widespread protests, with Conan O'Brien's late-night talk show devoting air-time to the closure. But the restaurant reopened in 2015 in this new location. Just before its reopening, proprietor David Ho told a reporter: "A long time ago, [Sam Wo's] was built from something bad [the 1906 quake] and something nice blossomed from it. The restaurant blooming again is something to look forward to."

1849

OLDEST CHINATOWN IN NORTH AMERICA

CHINATOWN

An area bounded, roughly, by Bush Street at south, Broadway at north, Kearny Street at east and Powell Street at west

The oldest Chinatown in North America can trace its roots to 1849, when four Chinese immigrant merchants held a meeting with 300 others at the Canton restaurant on Jackson Street. Their purpose was to persuade a local lawyer to speak for their community "in the event of unforeseen difficulties." And difficulties soon came—Chinatown's very existence is testimony to this group's persistence in the face of hostility. In the 1870s, demagogue Dennis Kearney whipped the Workingmen's Party into a fervor with cries of "The Chinese Must Go!" In 1882, the US Congress made this fear and loathing legal when it enacted a ban on further immigration from China—one of a long series of laws and court decisions that targeted the Chinese. And, when the 1906 quake and the resulting fire demolished Chinatown, some civic leaders proposed to shunt it to the city's southern fringes. But the community built back here, near the city's center—and built back quickly.

This is the Chinatown we see now, a quintessentially San Francisco concoction of buildings constructed using Western techniques, embroidered with Chinese motifs. (The most exuberant of these is the former Chinese Telephone Exchange, now a bank at 743 Washington Street. Essentially, it's a mid-rise office block in a pagoda costume.) In addition to presenting an image that appeals to tourists, the goal was to create a city within a city, one that could supply its occupants with all essential services, from schools to hospitals, from banks to funeral homes.

Even a casual observer will notice that Chinatown is a neighborhood packed with churches and temples. Here, on the top floor of a tenement building on picturesque Waverly Place, is a temple founded in the 1850s dedicated to the goddess Tien Hou. Because of her remit as a protector of sailors and travelers, many early arrivals gave thanks at this temple for safe passage across the Pacific. These were people whose beliefs tended to mix Taoism, Buddhism, Confucianism, and ancestor worship.

In 1916 California's first female architect, Julia Morgan, built a YWCA here, on the slope upwards from Chinatown to Knob Hill—and now it's the home of the Chinese Historical Society of America (965 Clay St.). It offers excellent tours and exhibitions; a recent one focused on San Francisco–born, martial artist-movie star Bruce Lee, also the subject of a big mural just off Chinatown's main drag, Grant Street.

Political struggles in China have long played out here also. In St. Mary's Square, a park near Chinatown's southern end, is a bust of Sun Yat-Sen, who raised funds to help overthrow the Ching dynasty, China's rulers from 1644. After his successful coup in 1911, the barbershops that once lined Waverly Place busied themselves cutting off the long, braided queues that symbolized allegiance to the emperor. Chinatown's long-term attachment to the nationalist cause is reflected in its very gates, a gift from Taiwan in 1969.

From the late 19th century until 1970, the police force had a squad of mainly White officers devoted to cracking down on Chinatown. It was a sign of the times when the force recently gained its first Chinese-American head, Fred Harry Lau. And in Edwin Lee San Francisco had its first Chinese-American mayor, from 2011 to his sudden death in 2017. Before becoming mayor, Lee worked in the urban-housing movement, whose push for affordable, decent housing remains relevant in today's Chinatown: It packs some 70,000 residents into a small area, making it one of the densest urban enclaves in North America.

A local food writer has aptly called Mr. Jiu's restaurant (28 Waverly Pl.) a love letter to Old Chinatown. In an homage to the most stylish cocktail bars and restaurants in Chinatown of yore, chef Brandon Jew serves food in a Cantonese-meets-Californian-Cuisine style. The whole package has earned a Michelin star. Together, the vibe and the dishes speak to a new generation's confidence and sophistication, a present born from this city-within-a-city's rich past.

Simpler fare is on offer at the country's oldest dim sum specialist, Hang Ah Tea House (1 Pagoda Pl.). It first opened in 1920, and the menu contains many dishes it helped popularize in North America, from shiu mai to potstickers, from bao stuffed with barbecued pork to garlic-accented bok choy It's a few steps off a side street, near the playground named for the basketball player Willy Wong.

1862

OLDEST ATHLETIC CLUB IN AMERICA

OLYMPIC CLUB

524 Post St.

"The business history of San Francisco could be written . . . with reference only to members of the Olympic Club." So writes historian Kevin Starr of this oldest athletic club in America. It's counted sugar kings, silver kings, and railway barons among its members. At least five mayors, a governor, and a chief justice of the Supreme Court have all belonged. It's also always had literary pretensions, with an in-house magazine and Mark Twain an early member. But for all that it is a real athletic club, with members who've reached the top tier of many sports.

The club was founded by two German-American artists, the half-brothers Arthur and Charles Christian Nahl. Both were members of the German gymnastics movement, founded in the early 19th century to pump up the youth after Napoleon's troops whipped them in the Battle of Jena. These two painted pictures of and for the gentry, and the club soon drew many of their high-rolling friends.

The club always found a way to ferret out athletic talent, sponsoring the training of those less financially endowed than its core membership. And so, though a young, handsome boxer named Jim Corbett was the son of a stableman and an assistant teller at the Nevada Bank, the club scouted him out and trained him, helping him to unseat the reigning world champion, John L. Sullivan.

Corbett's looks, the surprising delicacy of his hands, and his love of fancy dress earned him the nickname Gentleman Jim. He is credited with being the first boxer to jump up and down in his corner of the ring before beginning to box.

The club's top-tier coaches have always encouraged playing smart as well as hard. And so, at the turn of the 20th century, swimmer J. Scott Leary helped popularize an Australian stroke, that was, one observer said, "a bit like crawling through the water"—the front crawl. In the 1930s, club member and college-basketball star Angelo Luisetti helped make the one-armed hook shot a thing—impossible, now, to imagine the game without it. When the sport of pole-vaulting was young, member Cornelius Warmerdam, the so-called Flying Dutchman, earned himself (and his trainers) accolades for mastering so many skills. "He was," a contemporary commented, "part sprinter, part shock-absorber, part acrobat, part strongman."

Among its many Olympic champions, perhaps one has a particular claim on posterity. In the early 20th century, shot-putter Ralph Rose kept breaking his own world records, becoming the first to toss the shot over 50 feet. As flag-bearer for the Americans at the 1904 London Games, Rose caused a stir by not lowering his flag to the royal box. "This flag dips to no earthly king," he reportedly said.

In 1918, the club purchased the first of its now three golf courses, outside the city proper. It has since hosted five US Opens, with its challenging main course developing a reputation for giant-killing. Here a host of legends have fallen to relative unknowns, starting with Ben Hogan's upset by Jack Fleck in 1955. In 1966 Billy Casper beat Arnold Palmer; in 1987 Scott Simpson beat Tom Watson; and in 1998 Lee Janzen beat Payne Stewart.

In 2021, for the first time, the club hosted the women's US Open, with Filipino pro Yuka Sasso taking home the title. For years the club had refused to admit women or non-White athletes. And it spent over $1 million to fight a suit by the city attorney to force it to accept women before finally accepting its first female member in 1992.

"Many of its women's teams have become contenders," says club archivist Jessica Smith. "There have been national championships in soccer, basketball, field hockey."

Courtesy San Francisco History Center, San Francisco Public Library

1852

OLDEST BANK

WELLS FARGO

420 Montgomery St.

The men who cofounded what is now the nation's third-largest bank were from upstate New York, gentlemen who'd done well in the lucrative transport and shipping business. By 1850, Henry Wells had become president of American Express—the "express" spoke to the company's focus on moving parcels and money about fast. A man who'd go on to become mayor of Buffalo, William Fargo, then served as AmEx's corporate secretary. When these officers proposed to the board that AmEx expand to Gold Rush–era San Francisco, some directors balked, and Wells and Fargo decided to go it alone. Founded with $300,000 (just over $11 million in today's money), it is now worth upwards of $306 billion.

At the base of the bank's current corporate headquarters is a small museum, featuring the tiny, handheld scales used by the bank's early assayers to value the powder and nuggets dumped on the counters by miners who'd struck it rich. (Some of the nuggets on exhibit were stolen in 2014 by masked bandits, but the scales remain.) The museum has the oak boxes in which gold and important papers were carried, a Pony Express saddlebag, and a check for $1,000, payable to dry-goods merchant (later blue-jean salesman) Levi Strauss.

But its star attraction is one of the stagecoaches the bank once used to move money, mail, and passengers about. Pulled by six horses, such a vehicle could make it from Kansas City to San Francisco in 22 days. The Pony Express came into being to reduce that time. A succession of young men riding at breakneck speeds could get from Missouri to San Francisco in 10 days. Both coach and rider became outmoded, though, in 1869, with the completion of the transcontinental railway link. The postal service got into the business of delivering parcels in 1913, and Wells Fargo lost its lucrative shipping and handling work altogether in 1918 when Woodrow Wilson's government nationalized such activities. As a corporate history states: "It left Wells Fargo with one line of business—banking—and only one banking office, located in San Francisco."

Much of the bank's ongoing success is no doubt due to savvy management of risk—but Wells Fargo also has tended to adopt new technologies early. In the museum are the Morse code tappers used to send messages, by telegraph, between its then far-flung branches—on display is an 1853 message giving physical descriptions of some stagecoach robbers. Another 19th-century device on exhibit could copy documents, at least those written in iron-oxide ink.

Certain innovations introduced over the years would not take. Having a teller below street-level communicating, via tubes and mirrors, with drivers pulling up at a street-side kiosk—that didn't stick around. But others did, including the magnetic ink character recognition introduced in the late 1950s that helped machines identify and process checks; the introduction in the mid-1960s of a house credit card (from what was then Master Charge); and, in 1970, the launch of an early automatic teller machine. As befits a business with a big San Francisco presence, Wells Fargo was the first of the big players to offer Internet banking, in 1995.

In the new millennium the bank has grown by merger and acquisition. It has also tried to stake out a claim in the environmental sphere, investing in Green businesses, leading a group of banks seeking to make their operations carbon-neutral by the mid-century. Nevertheless, the often-sleepy museum recently drew a crowd of environmentalist protesters who locked themselves to various fixtures, hoping to convince the bank to cease backing fossil-fuel companies.

When the Wells Fargo stagecoaches carried valuable cargo, often a rifle-toting guard sat next to the driver—the origin, supposedly, of the phrase, "riding shotgun." One notorious bandit, known as Black Bart, pulled off 28 successful heists around the West. He was unfailingly polite to those he was sticking up, wore a bowler hat, and twice dropped poems at the scene of crime.

A telltale handkerchief, dropped during a heist finally gave him away. It had a San Francisco laundry's mark, and the bank's detective visited nearly 90 washhouses before linking it to a Civil War veteran, Charlie Boles. A few years prior, when prospecting for gold in Idaho and Montana, he'd had an unfortunate run-in with some Wells Fargo agents and swore he'd show them. For a time he did—but he ended up spending most of the rest of his life in San Quentin.

1908

OLDEST HEAD OFFICE OF THE BANK OF AMERICA

FIRST BANK OF AMERICA CORPORATE HEADQUARTERS

550 Montgomery St.

This 10-story Renaissance Revival building was commissioned by one of the great American businessmen of the first half of the 20th century, a dynamo who reinvented American banking practice and, in doing so, helped California become an economic powerhouse.

Amadeo Pietro Giannini was the son of two adventurous parents. His father Luigi left a small village near Genoa to try his luck in California's gold fields, doing well enough that he could afford to buy a 40-acre farm near San Jose. For a few years, the farm was successful, its produce coming by wagon up to an old market near the San Francisco waterfront. Unfortunately, Luigi was shot and killed by a laborer in a pay dispute. His wife Virginia, who was pregnant at the time, took over the farm, and then married a fruit and vegetable wholesaler who took 13-year-old Amadeo into the business.

The boy had a knack for it, and retired for the first time at age 31. His stepfather, now deceased, had left him an inheritance and a seat on the board of a local bank, the Columbus Savings & Loan. Giannini pushed the board to go after the business of the small farmers and business owners he'd met through his work at the market. When his fellow directors balked, he set up a competing bank in 1904. Within a year, his scrappy Bank of Italy had a respectable $700,000 on deposit.

When the earthquake hit, he managed to get his gold and currency out of town—some say it went in a garbage truck to his home in San Mateo, others in milk cans by boat across the Bay to Berkeley. Whatever the case, most of the other banks couldn't get at their vaults; even if they survived the fire, they remained too hot to open for weeks. Meanwhile, Giannini was back at the waterfront market, his desk a plank between two barrels, doling out money the survivors needed, making loans on a handshake.

He made such decisions, he said, by weighing up the character of the would-be borrowers, and he said every single one of these post-quake loans got repaid. It was with this money that he built headquarters in the heart of the financial district. But though most banks centralized their business in one big office, Giannini went to where his customers were, setting up branches in small towns across the state. In San Francisco, he had offices staffed by those who spoke Greek, Russian, Chinese, French, and, of course, Italian—as well as two operated mainly by women, catering to their financial needs.

In the 1920s, he merged with a Los Angeles bank that had grandly named itself the Bank of America. Thinking he'd rest on these laurels, he took his second retirement. But when the bank responded to the post-1929 economic crash by pulling back, he took charge again. He bet on the nascent film industry in LA, giving Walt Disney

the money to make his first full-length animated feature, *Snow White and the Seven Dwarves*, and backed the bonanza *Gone with the Wind*. (The idealistic banker in Frank Capra's *It's a Wonderful Life* is said to be based on Giannini.) Nearer to home, he invested in NorCal's young wine industry and the construction of the Golden Gate Bridge. After Pearl Harbor, he helped Henry Kaiser build the ships that would help win the war in the Pacific.

He also had the foresight to back two young would-be tech entrepreneurs, one named Bill Hewlett, the other David Packard. By the time he died in 1949, the Bank of America had become the world's largest commercial bank, with 500 branches and $6 billion in deposits.

In the 1920s, Giannini owned Transamerica, using it as a holding company for his various interests. It passed out of his hands, but in 1972, the insurance conglomerate would build its flagship office (600 Montgomery St.), just across the street from the relatively diminutive former Bank of Italy headquarters. Until the Salesforce Tower went up in 2017, this 48-story, pyramid-shaped skyscraper was the tallest building in the city, dwarfing the tall redwoods in the little park beside it. In his series Tales of the City, *novelist Armistead Maupin puts some of his characters to work in the Transamerica. Its presence helps ground his woo-woo comparison of San Francisco to the legendary lost city of Atlantis. He says it is only right that the modern city has its own pyramid, as Atlantis supposedly did; he worries aloud that his beloved San Francisco may, too, one day slip into the sea.*

1893

OLDEST GERMAN BEER HALL

SCHROEDER'S

240 Front St.

Henry Schroeder came from the Northern German port city Hamburg and began serving San Francisco's German immigrants (and others) from a first location at Market and Pine. There was a good-sized population of Germans in the city then; by 1860, they accounted for nearly 20 percent of the frontier city's population. According to scholar Carol Cosgrove Terry, they brought with them a desire to encourage merriment: "They taught their Anglo neighbors the importance of adding *Gemütlichkeit* into their daily lives."

Schroeder's has had Gemütlichkeit on tap from the get-go—along with plentiful beer to wash down the schnitzels and sausages. Even so, the place has had its trials over the years. The first location burned down after the 1906 quake, and Schroeder is credited with helping rebuild the downtown as a whole. Schroeder soldiered through a wave of anti-German feeling in WWI, but passed away soon after. His widow sold the bar in 1922 to another German-American, one Max Kniesche. Prohibition made it more than a little tricky to run a hofbrau.

Still, he managed, and had one of the longest tenures of any bar proprietor in San Francisco's boozy history, still running the place well into his 80s.

In 1939, another Hamburger, Herman Richter, an artist visiting the city, walked in and offered to cover the walls with murals. Most are cheeky, bawdy numbers—a young, strapping lad kissing his buxom girl, while two little kids titter away in some bushes, a woman dressed like an extra in *Cabaret*, astride a huge bottle of champagne.

But one thing Schroeder's didn't have, at least at lunch, was female customers. In 1970, Kniesche and his staffers twice turned away a woman named Carol Weintraub. Big mistake. Weintraub worked as the director of the Northern California chapter of the American Civil Liberties Association and promptly launched a suit, seeking damages and a change in the exclusion policy. Kniesche shot back: "If we have women in here, I'll lose 80 percent of my customers. . . . If a woman comes in, she wants something light and dainty. She wouldn't like the food I serve." His comments were reported, someone smashed a window, and an anonymous caller said that Kniesche was "A *Schweinhund*." Kniesche caved.

Schroeder's passed from owner to owner after Kniesche's family sold it in 1990. It looked to be on its last legs when Andy Chun and Jan Wiginton purchased it just over a decade ago. In a reported $1-million revamp, they replaced the linoleum floors with oak and ditched the red pleather-upholstered seats in favor of long communal tables and benches typical of many German beerhalls. The dirndls on the female waitstaff? *Nein, danke.*

But the murals they let be, along with the old rosewood bar, which came to San Francisco in the 1880s, shipped around Cape Horn. The look now is cleaner, with just a stag's head here, a boar's head there. When the World Cup comes on, a digital projector drops down and it becomes one of the best places in the city to take in the games. *Sehr gemütlich.*

Working with a German-Californian chef, the pair also reworked the menu. Now Schroeder's serves iconic German fare, but also a vegetal Beyond Bratwurst sausage. That mitteleuropean specialty spätzle is on offer, but the grated-potato dish has tomatoes, corn, ricotta, and onion blossoms mixed in.

A sign reads, "Ladies and Gentlemen for lunch and dinner" making it clear Schroeder's now welcomes all to do shots of Jäger and munch on giant pretzels. Says Chun, "It's nice, given the history, that the restaurant is now half-owned by a woman."

1849

OLDEST RESTAURANT

TADICH GRILL

240 California St.

Founded in 1861 and still in the same spot, the Old Clam House sometimes disputes the Tadich Grill's claim to be the oldest local restaurant. Certainly, Tadich has gone by several names—the New World Coffee Stand, the New World Saloon, and The Cold Day Restaurant among them. It has also occupied no fewer than eight locations.

But there's been enough continuity to bolster the Tadich claim. It's always been owned and operated by Croatian-American families. And, though it's jumped around some, it's always chosen to locate near the heart of the city. There also appears to have been legal continuity throughout.

The logo on the menu and crockery identifies the place as "The Original Cold Day Restaurant." One might think that this is attempt, through branding, to draw customers in when it's chilly outside. But the name has a specific origin story. One of the Grill's early regulars was Alexander Badlam Jr., known as Boisterous Badlam. As a young man, he mined in Amador County, but back-breaking toil was not his thing. He became a state legislator and then the County of San Francisco's assessor. He ran to get reelected to this office with the slogan, It'll be a Cold Day Before I Leave. That bit of presumption helped get him tossed, with voters unloading a carriage full of ice on his stoop for good measure. You want a cold day; we'll give you a cold day.

He and his cronies often ate here and perhaps they were served, from time to time, by John Tadich himself. A Croatian immigrant, he joined the staff in 1871 and eventually bought the place, naming it The Cold Day. Then his partner, a fellow ex-pat named John Sutich, struck out on his own and used the same name for his new establishment. A furious Tadich asserted his rights, with the tagline, The Original Cold Day Restaurant, one that remains years after Sutich's upstart restaurant closed.

Another crowd of Croatians took over in the late 1920s, the Buich Brothers, Tom, Mitch, and Louie, and their successors still run the place. Louie gets credited with the Tadich's main contribution to the American culinary scene: He supposedly began grilling fish and meats in the old Croatian style, over mesquite charcoal, and popularized that now common mode of cooking in the New World. Today, the wine list leads with a chardonnay from Wente—one of California's oldest wineries—and beer from the oldest brewery, Anchor Steam, is on tap. These drinks can wash down solid renditions of San Francisco's classic dishes: its seafood stew (Cioppino), its oyster-accented frittata (the Hangtown Fry), its crab salad (the Louie), and the local catches that dominate the menu (sand dabs, Petrale sole, and Dungeness crab).

In 1967, the Tadich Grill moved from Clay Street and settled down in its current location. But it feels like it's been here forever.

The waiters wear white jackets, black slacks, and dark ties. An 80-foot-long bar, perfect for solo meals, stretches the length of the place, while there are wood-paneled booths for larger parties, with curtains, stained-glass accents, and old buttons to call for service. (They don't work anymore.) In fact, a designer did such a good job of mimicking the old Deco fixtures that, after the first lunch in the new place, regulars reportedly rose to applaud.

Current owner Mike Buich started working here at age 9, peeling shrimp and bussing tables. In this future-oriented town, he recently told SFGATE: "There's a novelty to tradition in today's society." It'll be a cold day, indeed, when the Tadich closes.

Just around the corner from the Tadich is the oldest stationery shop in the city, Patrick & Co. (560 Market St.). If you still pencil appointments in to your leather-bound Lett's of London diary, this is your place. If you know how to write a bread-and-butter thank-you note, you can buy watermarked Crane's stationery here.

Moise-Klinker Co. hung out its shingle in 1873, advertising, "Business Supplies and Rubber Stamps." In 1890, a traveling salesman, James Patrick, began working in the field, and four generations followed him, creating a powerhouse that gobbled up Moise-Klinker and other small stationery stores. Though it now has an online presence and earns most of its keep by providing supplies to large businesses, the flagship location of Patrick & Co. has every little thing that those with fussy, old-school leanings could want for their offices.

1854

OLDEST MEMBERS' LIBRARY AND CHESS CLUB

MECHANICS' INSTITUTE

57 Post St.

The movement that founded Mechanics' Institutes all over the world started in Scotland in the 1820s. Branches of the Institute attempted to provide a technical education to those unable to afford (or get into) university, while also aiming to enrich the cultural lives of their members. The early union slogan, "Give us bread, but give us roses also," encapsulates the Institute's early mission.

It touched down in San Francisco a few years after the first gold strikes inland, at a time when the city was awash with unemployed miners. From the start, it was open to men and women of any race, charging a modest fee. Browsers could go right into the stacks—many other libraries at that time required you to place an order for a specific book at a desk. These were radical ideas at the time.

The Institute was able to keep fees low because of benefactors like James Lick. This Pennsylvania-born cabinet- and piano-maker came here in the late 1840s and foresaw the coming boom, buying up land all over the state. His money helped fund free public baths; the local chapter of the Society for the Prevention of Cruelty to Animals; two orphanages; a co-ed school; an observatory; an asylum for poor, elderly women; and, yes, to endow the Institute. Andrew Hallidie, who invented the cable car, also gave to the Institute, and

to libraries in general. The Institute had one of the largest collection of books, locally, until he helped get the city's public library going in 1879.

The Institute has also hosted one of the country's oldest, continuously operating chess clubs. Some say an appreciation for the game was seeded here in the 1850s by the French consul to the city, Pierre Saint-Amant, one of the world's best players. Certainly, the Institute has since provided a home for local enthusiasts and attracted such champions as Boris Spassky and Bobby Fischer. In 1920, the club hosted what librarian and historian Taryn Edwards now calls its first virtual event, with local players communicating their moves, by telegraph, to others in Southern California. The Chess Club's Tuesday-night marathons pit players of all ages and skill levels against each other over the course of several matches.

"The game helps our younger members, the kids, especially, to think strategically and be good sports," the Institute's former head Kimberly Scrafano says. "This is whether they go on to compete or not." (Many do: One of its members, 12-year-old Daniel Naroditsky, won the World Championship in his age group in 2009 and has gone on to compete at the game's top levels.) Scrafano adds: "We had a surge in interest in it from girls and women after [the popular TV show] *The Queen's Gambit* came out." The club offers classes in the game.

A map on one wall shows an imaginative version of the city, in the year of the Institute's founding, 1854. It shows both existing and imagined future streets. There's an optimism breathing in it, the sort of can-do feeling the Institute has long sought to foster.

A few blocks from the Institute, at the intersection of Market, Bush, and Battery Streets, sits the splendid Mechanics' Monument, one of three major sculptures along the city's main drag done by a deaf artist Douglas Tilden. A local boy who trained in Paris, Tilden presented a statue of a baseball player to the French, at a big salon—and they loved it. He completed this paean to the working man at the turn of the 20th century. It was dedicated in 1901 by then-mayor James Phelan, and features five separate, nearly nude men, operating, together, a punching machine, straining their well-defined muscles as they work. (Some local prudes proposed to put trousers on them, but they were ignored.)

The statue came through the post-quake fire relatively unscathed, the photos of it against a burned-out cityscape representing to many the spirit the disaster could not destroy.

1852

OLDEST JEWELER

SHREVE & CO.

150 Post St.

The Shreves were a Boston family involved in the jewelry trade, and two of them, George and his nephew Samuel, headed west during the Gold Rush. In 1852, they established what was initially a retail operation, not far from their current location in the city's glam shopping district Union Square. Samuel died, reportedly drowning near Panama, and George shifted the focus from selling trinkets to making them, starting to manufacture fine silverware sometime after the discovery of the Comstock Lode in Nevada in 1859.

Courtesy Shreve & Co.

Gold Rush-era San Francisco was a rough-and-tumble, ultra-masculine town—men vastly outnumbering women—and early on Shreve began to specialize in men's timepieces. In 1887, it became the second American jeweler to represent Swiss watchmaker Patek Philippe, a brand it still represents today. At the turn of the century, it began the process of building its headquarters, an 11-story building at the corner of Post and Grant. It was completed in 1906.

The building took a licking from the quake and the fire, but, like those timepieces, kept on ticking. It survived, as did the inventory that was stored in a big vault.

The reopened store soon became the place where fancy folk went to buy engagement, wedding, and anniversary rings. The jeweler also created big, one-off pieces for collectors—things like a life-sized gold rooster and a 10-inch tall, solid-gold teddy bear for (who else) Teddy Roosevelt, who began the plush teddy bear craze. It made a silver spade used by President William Howard Taft to break ground for the 1915 Panama-Pacific International Exhibition here and another one for mayor James Rolph to give a ceremonial start to the construction of San Francisco City Hall. By then, the firm had been purchased by the family of longtime staffer Albert Lewis.

Shreve's present owner is the North Carolina–based Schiffman and Co., established in 1892. It's run by three brothers, and one of them, Lane Schiffman, has taken a special interest in the San Francisco firm. As Schiffman tells it, sourcing the best jewels has become a global game. "We go all over, getting diamonds mined in South Africa, Botswana and Israel, rubies from Madagascar, emeralds from Colombia, opals from Australia. Pearls you get from Indonesia and a different kind from Japan. Thailand is the world capital of sapphires and Afghanistan is a great source of Lapis."

He says there was a small dip in watch sales when many began using their smartphones to tell time, but, after the introduction of the Apple Watch, he saw a rebound in high-end watch sales. "It was like they had something on their wrist again, they got used to using it again, and thought that's sort of nice, having the time there." In the casual Bay Area, a high-end watch has become one of the few financial flexes that the tech gods allow themselves—that and a high-end Tesla.

Schiffman says staff are trained not to assess customers based on their appearance. "We never judge a book by its cover. That's especially important in San Francisco, where you get some guy with a pony tail, in jeans and a T-shirt, and he looks at something for a bit, some amazing thing, and says, you know, yeah I want that, I'll take it. As a set of small stores, we make our way . . . by building relationships. By being the exact opposite of Amazon." In a sign of post-millennial San Francisco's sustained boom, Shreve no longer bothers carrying silver—now, as during the city's infancy, gold is where it's at.

You sometimes hear that Dashiell Hammett, author of the Sam Spade mystery novels, once worked for Shreve. Given that his book, The Maltese Falcon, *relates to a famous bird-shaped jewel gone missing in San Francisco, you can see how the rumor began. But I could find no evidence to support his having worked in the high-end shop.*

Still, Shreve & Co. is the focus of Hammett walking tours, which also feature John's Grill (63 Ellis St.), just a few blocks away The booth-filled restaurant still features Sam Spade's order in the Falcon—lamb chops, roasted potato, and sliced tomato. Upstairs, there's a replica of the bird used in the 1941 film starring Humphrey Bogart. After that, you can walk a few blocks to a plaque on dead-end Burritt St. that treats a climactic event in the novel as real: "On approximately this spot," it reads, "Miles Archer, partner of Sam Spade, was done in by Brigid O'Shaughnessy"

1964

OLDEST DEPARTMENT STORE

GUMP'S

250 Post St.

There are only vestiges of the old, family-run department stores that once surrounded Union Square and made it one of the world's great shopping destinations. Two of them, the City of Paris and the White House, looked mainly to France for inspiration. Another, I. Magnin, capitalized on the sewing skills of the family's Dutch-American matriarch. But the most quintessentially San Francisco of the bunch was Gump's—and so, perhaps, it's appropriate that it is the only one still going.

The first Gumps to run the store were the brothers Solomon and Gustave, Jewish immigrants from Heidelberg. With their sister's husband, they began selling gilded mirrors to saloons and brothels and the Nob Hill mansions of the newly rich. A high-low mix would become the brand for Gump's—"naughty with class," as one local observed.

This two-step was apparent in the Gumps' move into art, with their gallery, the city's first, showing fine paintings acquired in Europe, as well as nudes of Solomon's mistress—at least, that's what the family said, maybe in jest. But art was never a joking matter at Gump's, which exhibited and sold canvases by the likes of Rembrandt, Picasso, Robert Motherwell, and Willem de Kooning as well as local stars Wayne Thiebaud and Richard Diebenkorn.

Early in the 20th century, Solomon's son Abraham took over, heading Gump's when the earthquake hit in 1906. It was a well-known madam, Dodie Valencia, who reportedly helped in the reboot, buying a painting from Abraham for some $17,000. In an era when acting on the stage was still considered outré, Abraham's actress wife Mabel both burnished and tarnished the family name by appearing onstage in a string of Gump's pearls while flanked by wolfhounds.

It was Abraham (or "A.I.," as he came to be known) who sent buyers to Japan and China to source jewelry, porcelain, and woodblock prints. Despite poor eyesight, he became such a connoisseur of jade that he was able to tell much about a carved stone's quality by touch. Eleanor Roosevelt bought some jade cups and saucers at Gump's and then gave them to the Duchess of Kent. Presiding over Gump's Asian galleries from 1928 was a large gilt Buddha from the Ch'ing dynasty. It would become a symbol of the store, what one observer called the "hush, plush cloister of impeccable taste."

Enter the next generation. A.I.'s son Richard was as obsessed with design as his father had been. He had once worked in Hollywood as a set designer and composer, and later conducted a jokey oom-pah-pah band and hosted a radio show. It was his older brother Robert who designed the store's logo, still in use today. After Robert left Gump's, he bummed around Mexico and penned a trippy volume of poetry, *You are the Rose, You are the Rock*—it was popular with hippies in the 1960s. His third marriage, to another San Francisco madam, Sally Stanford, generated headlines. Naughty with class.

Throughout, the store's design-savvy staff carried on. The unveiling of Gump's Christmas windows was a civic event. Inside, there was a room devoted to jade, as well as what the store liked to call its Great Wall of China. This plate-lined feature made Gump's the place for well-to-do brides to choose table settings.

In 1969, the family sold the store, and since then it has limped along with various owners. The Buddha has left the building, auctioned off by Christie's for $4 million. And it remains to be seen if the new ownership can find a way to reinvent Gump's with e-commerce on the march. In a sign of these changed times, an Apple Store now dominates one side of Union Square.

Another vestige of these grand local department stores is the opalescent dome in the current-day Neiman Marcus (150 Stockton St.). It was saved from the City of Paris store, and features, in stained glass, a ship with the motto "Fluctuat nec mergitur" *("it may rock but never sinks.") But sink the store did, closing in 1972, after over 120 years in operation.*

Like Gump's, the City of Paris was founded by two brothers, Émile and Félix Verdier, from a family that owned a silk-stocking outfit in France. The stained-glass window was one of the crowning glories of the store's post-quake home. Despite local opposition (to the tune of 60,000 signatures on a petition), despite the 1909 building earning a spot on the National Register of Historic Places, the company that owns Neiman Marcus felt it needed too many repairs. In 1983, it put up, in its stead, Philip Johnson's flashy, checkerboard-sided building, integrating the glass dome into the design.

1875

OLDEST HOTEL

PALACE HOTEL

2 New Montgomery St.

Portraits of the two different men who made this hotel happen hang behind the long mahogany reception desk, at either end. This distance is appropriate, considering the circumstances that left the hotel founded by the one man in the other's possession.

An Ohioan, William Chapman Ralston came to the city during the Gold Rush, and worked for Cornelius Vanderbilt's shipping company. With the proceeds, he helped found the Bank of California in 1864, hiring William Sharon to run a branch near a silver strike in Nevada. Sharon did well by the bank, taking shares in mining concerns as collateral for loans and foreclosing swiftly on defaults.

Courtesy Palace Hotel

As the money came pouring in, Ralston used much of it to fund ambitious buildings in his adopted city. His pet project was the Palace, for which he secured an entire block on the city's main street of Market Street. With $5 million, he built seven stories and 755 rooms, each with a marble fireplace. Meanwhile, Sharon quietly sold off his mining stock and made Ralston's own shares nearly worthless. With debts due, Ralston turned to Sharon for help. Sharon bailed him out, but, repeating his strategy with the miners, took ownership of every last thing of Ralston's, including the Palace.

Ruined, Ralston was last seen swimming from North Beach towards Alcatraz. He never came back. But Sharon, his former partner, would go on to live (and die) at the Palace, as well as conduct a notorious affair with a woman in the hotel across the street, the considerably less grand Grand Hotel.

The Palace weathered this scandal, and it made it through the 1906 quake—but, sadly, not the ensuing fire. Appropriately, the new hotel that rose from the ashes in 1909 had a phoenix as its logo. And at least one feature of Ralston's hotel returned—the canopy of stained glass that covers the current-day Garden Court, which still hosts the West's oldest debutante ball.

Where people in other cities put on the Ritz, San Francisco locals come to the Palace to get fancy. So do guests from afar. Here have stayed aviators Charles Lindbergh and Amelia Earhart, inventors Thomas Edison and Guglielmo Marconi, and royals from Princess Juliana of Holland to England's Prince Philip. One of the 18 presidents to visit, Warren Harding died in his suite in 1923, under suspicious circumstances. (His wife's refusal to allow an autopsy still fuels the rumor that she poisoned him.) And in the lobby, across from the Garden Court, are two scarlet-and-gold thrones, a gift to the hotel from Hawaii to reflect the passing of David Kalakaua, last king of the islands, in his Palace room.

Descendants of Sharon's sold the Palace in the 1950s to the Sheraton chain, which, in turn, passed it on to its current owner, Kyo-Ya, in the 1970s. This Japanese-Hawaiian hotel management company was midway through a big renovation when the 1989 Loma Prieta quake hit. Finished in 1991, this respectful $150-million rework added another glass-canopied space towards the rear of the hotel. Floating in the pool beneath it, one can look up at skyscrapers representing most of the 20th century's main architectural movements.

Highlights of the hotel's own century and a half are contained in a lively mini-museum where the telephone switchboard used to be. Near the lobby, glass cases show off the hotel's period sterling, an appropriate display for a hotel founded by two silver kings. One is remembered as a visionary, the other as a rogue who executed on his partner's visions and reaped profits from what the other had sown.

The bar across from the Palace's main entry, the House of Shields (39 New Montgomery St.), opened in 1908, just around the time the second Palace got up and running. Though it sounds like a lesser-known tarot card, it's actually named for an early proprietor, Eddie Shields, whose usual description as "a boxing-world associate" is somehow evocative. A speakeasy during Prohibition, the House supposedly had a tunnel to the Palace, allowing thirsty guests to come and go surreptitiously. The city was—and remains—one of the capitals of neon, and here the sign, spelling out the bar's name in red light, recalls one of the Humphrey Bogart movies set in San Francisco. Inside there is, deliberately, no clock. And the House does feel out of time—or at least not in the now—with its wood panelling, liveried bartenders, and menu of classic cocktails.

1918

OLDEST GLASS CURTAIN WALL

HALLIDIE BUILDING

130 Sutter St.

This late work by architect Willis Polk has, arguably, the first real glass curtain wall to front a building in America—nearly four decades before the technique became commonplace. Completed in 1918 and commissioned by the University of California, it has a vast, reflective surface, trimmed in Cal's colors, gold and blue. At seven stories, it's an elegant building, with Juliet balconies curving round the fire-escapes. "It's taught at most architectural schools," says Craig Hartman, who recently designed the International Terminal at the San Francisco Airport. "Its transparency and delicacy are amazing." (Though named for Andrew Hallidie, the local inventor who pioneered the cable car, it has no specific connection to him.)

Polk was born in Illinois and studied in Columbia's well-regarded architecture program. Early on, he worked with some leading architects, including Chicago-based skyscraper specialist Daniel Burnham. He headed Burnham's office in San Francisco and co-designed the Merchants' Exchange Building (465 California St.). Completed in 1903, it has a facade of Tennessee granite and veined marble in the lobbies—all opulence in the Beaux-Arts style. Polk's 1914 skyscraper, the Hobart Building (582 Marke St.) clocked in at 21 floors, with neoclassical embellishment. Both were deluxe, even heavy additions to the cityscape.

The relative lightness of the Hallidie building represents a departure from these two, making a claim on Polk's behalf that he became, at the end of his career, the city's first modernist.

But Polk had always seemed like someone who might do his own thing, a brewing rebellion. He disdained his adopted city's Victorian homes ("architectural nightmares conceived in a reign of terror") and slammed the Richardsonian Romanesque style as "titanic inebriation in sandstone". "Obnoxious" was one local verdict on him. "A cowboy" was the more generous take.

Still, the Hallidie is really the only Polk building that markedly departs from other buildings of the day. Its budget was small for a downtown structure ($250,000), discouraging the ornamentation he'd larded on his other works. (It isn't quite without decoration, though, with delicate zinc flowers and birds, painted gold, in the trim at top and bottom.) Where he got the inspiration is still debated, but Polk often said that his own glass building owed something to the legendary Crystal Palace at the 1851 London exhibition. Maybe so, but the newer building takes full advantage of technologies not available in the mid-19th century.

The cagey man called it his Munchausen Building—a reference to a fantastical story in an 18th-century novel that has mad Baron von Munchausen pulling a bear inside out. Here the building's structural elements are concealed, its hefty reinforced concrete load-bearing walls hidden within. Early critics struggled to find the words to describe it, calling it, with some offense intended, the Camouflage Building, the Frontless Building, and the Daylight Building. Unfortunately, Polk passed away just a few years after its completion, long before the building became a site for architectural tourists to check off their lists.

Over the years, the Hallidie Building suffered from neglect, plagued by rust, warping glass, and chunks of missing trim. Elisa Hernandez Scaggs, an associate principal at the architectural firm Page & Turnbull, was one of several architects and contractors who worked on a restoration, finished in 2013. She had artisans replace lost elements in the trim and backed the delicate zinc panels with fiberglass. The old windows were replaced with new ones made of tough but attractive laminated glass.

"It was such a joy to work on this," she says. She goes on to call the building, "Innovative for him, innovative for San Francisco. There is no other building in the city like it. You could feel he had found the confidence to do just what he wanted."

Appropriately enough, the local chapter of the American Institute of Architects has recently moved into the lower floors of the Hallidie Building, renovating a former clothing store to put in a gallery and lecture hall. (The design is appropriately clean-lined, with big windows on the street, and was overseen by a leading San Francisco firm, Aidlin Darling.) The American Institute for Graphic Arts is also listed as a partner, making this a hub for design professionals. He might have disliked much of their work, but Willis Polk would certainly be happy that his late-career opus in glass and steel, his seven-story aviary, has drawn such birds to it.

Pro Tip: The best view of the Hallidie Building is to be had from the patio, accessible to the public, on top of the shopping arcade across the street, the Crocker Galleria (50 Post St.).

1939

OLDEST MENSWEAR STORE

CABLE CAR CLOTHIERS

110 Sutter St.

A portrait of a young Queen Elizabeth presides over this gentleman's haberdashery, one that has seen out the slovenly beatniks and the outré hippies, and, so far, has survived the ultra-casual tech revolution. Says nattily dressed Jonathan Levin, the third generation to run the business, "We're not cashmere hoodies—we're just cashmere."

Also looking down from the walls of this packed but tidy boutique is Levin's grandfather, its founder and presiding spirit, Charles Pivnick, known to Levin as The Boss. The son of Jewish immigrants from Eastern Europe, Pivnick worked as a newspaper boy in the 1920s and used to gawk in front of Hasting's, one of the stores that once dressed San Francisco's men, coveting the fine suits in the window.

After serving in WWII, Pivnick got into the clothing game with an army-surplus store, and then shifted to proper gentlemen's clothing. To help firm up his place in the market, he purchased Robert Kirk, an Anglo men's and women's clothing boutique. As for the store's name, one early outlet of Pivnick's stood near the corner of Powell and O'Farrell Streets, just at the crossing of two cable cars.

The 1950s and '60s were the glory days. Somehow, Pivnick expanded to a number of outlets while coaching a boys' basketball team for his synagogue and studying at night for his master's degree in marketing. "He had so much energy," Levin says. "He walked and took the bus here into his 90s, always dressed immaculately." (Born in 1919, Pivnick passed away in 2014.)

In addition to its several brick-and-mortar stores, Pivnick, with the help of Levin's mother Patricia, put out a catalog that had, at its height, a circulation of 2 million. Meanwhile, Pivnick's wife Janice and daughter Barri (Levin's aunt) grew the ladies' wear side of things, bringing in Liberty of London scarves and women's Burberry trenches. By this point, Pivnick had a closet of the kind of suits he'd longed for as a boy.

But in post-millennial San Francisco, many of the freshly minted tech billionaires prefer to dress down—way down. Now found in only one location, Cable Car has reverted to its original focus, menswear. Here, overlooked by Spy caricatures, are pocket squares and ascots; fancy-headed walking sticks and umbrellas; fedoras and flat caps; cufflinks and tie pins; tartan trousers and bowties; loafers, Oxfords, and the shoehorns to help ease into them. And, since it's not just clothes that maketh the man, the store also stocks old-school grooming products like tortoise-shell Kent combs and badger-hair shaving-cream brushes.

Over the years, the popular descriptors of the stock have changed, from proper to preppie, from Ivy League (Levin's preferred term) to, now, trad. "We have changed some with the times," says Levin, who helped build the store's online presence. And in with the classic shoes are some fancy sneakers that could work both with formal and informal outfits. Asked about popular athleisure wear, he says drily, "No, we haven't gone in for that." Standing near the front counter, he adds, "We're still focused on quality, on a wardrobe as an investment." As a sign of these times, he mentions the passing of the WASP-beloved Brooks Brothers chain. "We're the last survivor in San Francisco of the independent menswear stores, the oldest in the West. There are maybe a dozen other stores like us around the country."

The core proposition of the business is something Leven heard his grandfather say: "You have to deliver a good product and be kind to people."

Levin likes to eat around the corner at Sam's Grill (374 Bush St.). The Sam in question, one Sam Zenovich, was its proprietor in the 1920s and '30s. But its roots go even further back, to an oyster bar started in 1867. You'll still see seafood on the menu, alongside refreshments pioneered nearby, from Green Goddess dressing (on a wedge salad) to the Hangtown Fry (an oyster-accented egg dish). And the look is classic, with curtained booths, black-and-white photos on the walls, and uniformed waiters.

One of them, the courtly Stefano Crivello, helped put together the consortium of regulars who saved Sam's from closing in 2014—along with its former maitre d' and now co-owner Peter Quartaroli. Says Quartaroli: "It's always drawn interesting, unpretentious people. One of the 49ers coaches would come here back in the day, further back, boxer Jack Dempsey, Clint Eastwood when he was filming in town."

1875

OLDEST PUBLIC MONUMENT

LOTTA'S FOUNTAIN

Geary and Market Sts.

This, the oldest public monument in the city, is a tribute to the energies of several female troupers of the highest order.

We can thank Lotta Crabtree for its creation. Born in 1867, she began performing at the age of 6 in the theaters and saloons of Gold Rush–era Northern California. She learned about singing and dancing from the actress and courtesan Lola Montez, her neighbor in Grass Valley, a town in the California interior. But her first big break, in San Francisco, was due to Rowena Granice Steele, a writer, performer, and female-suffrage advocate who ran the evocatively named Temple of Mirth and Song. There, Steele and her son would often perform scenes from Shakespeare together, in addition to convening a variety show. The girls and young women who hoofed and sang the various numbers, Lotta among them, were called the Gaieties.

If Lotta's mentors were powerful women, she soon outstripped them all, touring her own theatre company across the continent. She excelled in stage versions of Dickens's most tearjerking novels—one of her signature roles was Little Nell. Petite into adulthood, this strong, driven woman made her way by playing vulnerable girls and ingénues well into middle age. In lighter entertainments, she was apt to stick a finger into a dimple. By the

1880s she was earning some $5,000 per week—about $135,000 in today's dollars, the equivalent of $7 million per annum. Diamonds weren't this girl's best friend—she preferred to spend on racehorses and bonds. When she retired in 1889, she was still on top, going out while still in demand.

Though she lived most of her life on the East Coast, Lotta retained a fondness for her hometown, giving it this gold-colored fantasia, replete with lions' heads and plaques of miners and sailing ships. (Its design is said to be based on a lighthouse that appeared as a prop in one of her plays.) Under the gilt patina, there is iron—a decent metaphor for Lotta herself— the entirety cast in Philadelphia and shipped around Cape Horn.

After the earthquake in 1906, Lotta's Fountain became a meeting point for those separated from from their loved ones, much like certain corners in New York after 9/11.

Another powerhouse, the Italian soprano Luisa Tetrazzini, gave a performance here on Christmas Eve, 1910, and a plaque with her likeness on it was added. The story passed down about that concert is that two agents believed they had the exclusive right to book her, and one, in the squabble, proposed to seek an injunction against her performing until it was decided. This open-air concert was her act of defiance.

Lotta herself returned to San Francisco for the Pan-Pacific International Exposition in 1915, the city's signal to the world that it was back, participating in a public ceremony here on a day that was named in her honor.

From 1924 on, survivors of the earthquake in 1906 would gather here on April 18 to mark the event. And though these survivors are now gone, a few historically minded people still do pilgrimages here throughout the day, often leaving wreaths.

Lotta died in 1924 in Boston. She gave that city a curious statue—a sculpture of a dog with a cat's face, placed in a wading pool. In the end, she left an estate valued at $4 million (roughly $65 million today), much of which would go to charities helping veterans, aging actors, and ex-convicts. Although she was a person of substance, the *New York Times* obituary would sum her up as "the eternal child." In 1951, Mitzi Gaynor played a freehand approximation of Lotta in the film musical *Golden Girl*.

1873

OLDEST CABLE CAR SYSTEM

CABLE CAR BARN AND POWERHOUSE

1201 Mason St.

The quintessential San Francisco conveyance, the cable car, was introduced to the city by an enterprising Scotsman named Andrew Hallidie. His father, an inventor, was the holder of 30 patents, including one for rope made of wire. His son also had faith in the potential of wire. At age 19 he introduced a device called the Endless Ropeway, a loop of wire that carried containers from the depths of the mines to a processing site. He also had guts, and showed it in the high country, where he weathered a winter storm that snowed him in for a month, kept his head when he got buried in a 600-foot tunnel, and survived a drop in a river that swept him half a mile downstream. Both qualities—ingenuity and guts—would come into play to make the cable car happen.

After proving the utility of his wire ropes, Hallidie set up a factory to make them. Then, in 1869, he witnessed some horses trying to haul a carriage up a steep hill. One of them slipped, and the cart rolled back down, dragging the horses after it. A founder of the local branch of the Society for the Prevention of Cruelty to Animals, Hallidie proposed a new version of his Endless Ropeway, replacing the container with a passenger car and attaching it to a subterranean wire loop. On a late summer night in 1873, he stood in a prototype car on a hilltop. The driver he hired balked at the

slope, and so he drove the car himself, careening down Clay Street to the bottom of a 307-foot drop. The grade was not gradual. At the bottom, Hallidie released, then braked, then attached to the wire loop again, mounting back to the summit in triumph.

That fall, Hallidie's cars began taking their first passengers on board, and lines soon proliferated across the city. One result of their success was a rush to develop the city's previously hard-to-access hilltops. (For instance, mansions sprang up in now-exclusive Nob Hill.) Cable cars spread to other cities, too.

The cars dominated for about a decade. Then electric street cars and diesel buses replaced them on all but the most hilly of their routes. Shortly after WWII, mayor Roger Lapham proposed to retire these survivors of a bygone era—all the other cities had already done so.

But then a socialite named Friedel Krussmann got involved. She and her fellow members of the San Francisco Flower Society distributed flyers around the city. With help from Richard Gump, the department store owner, she took out an ad in *Time* magazine. Then, over the mayor's objections, they put the fate of the cars up for a vote, winning in a landslide. In the late 1950s, a television ad for Rice-a-Roni featured a cable car and solidified the association between San Francisco and these vehicles.

Many of the first cars were lost in the earthquake and fire of 1906, but one of the originals was being shown off at a Baltimore fair. That car currently lives in the museum housed in the working Cable Car Barn and Powerhouse. The museum has big wheels that pull the descendants of Hallidie's wire loops, pulling the yesteryear cars around the city. Some cars are double-ended, so they can go either way with equal facility, while others have a definite front and back, and rotate on massive turntables at each end of their route. Another car, the number 19, recently came out of an epic 77-year retirement, lovingly restored, to become the oldest working car in San Francisco—it was completed in the technology's heyday in 1883.

The city is heaven for transit-history buffs, who gawk and geek out at the parade of retro vehicles on the annual Muni Heritage Day, with some volunteering at the San Francisco Railway Museum & Gift Shop (77 Steuart St.). But locals tend to be less bullish on the agency that runs them, the San Francisco Municipal Railway, known as the Muni, and called the Muniserable by kvetchers.

Part of the problem may be that the Muni began under a shadow, established in reaction to the 1908 conviction of lobbyist Abe Ruef for bribing the mayor while trying to secure a transit contract for a client. As a result, the first public transit agency to serve a major American city was born in 1912. Today, the Muni's services (though often the subject of local complaints) compare favorably to those in many other cities. In a big step forward, it recently streamlined a confusing fare system with a single mode of paying.

1912

OLDEST FOOTRACE

BAY TO BREAKERS

Start: Mission St. and Embarcadero

For many years, this was a small event with a no-nonsense name, the Cross-City Race. First run on New Year's Day, 1912, the race was won by Bobby Vlught, a student at the East Bay college St. Mary's. He managed to get from the edge of the San Francisco Bay to the breakers at Ocean Beach in just over 44 minutes. The times have come down since then—Kenyan runner Sammy Kitwara completed it in 2009 in the record time of 33 minutes, 31 seconds—and the character of the event has evolved.

Officially open to men only until 1971, there was some excitement when a top competitor's girlfriend, Barbara Burke, ran the race in 1941, outwitting the registrar by entering as Bobby. But mainly, for its first half century the race was a quiet, little event. In 1963 a mere 25 runners competed. In the next two decades it benefited from a catchy new name, the *San Francisco Examiner*'s publicity, and the growing mass obsession with jogging. A whopping 110,000 ran the 1986 race, setting a Guinness Book–certified world record.

But it was more than just the event's size and name that changed. As one recent writer commented: "The race took on . . . kookier qualities, a reputation for being more of a frat-party walk-a-thon and excuse for very early day drinking."

Costumes have long been a key part of the kookiness. The first recorded runner to sport one was a 1940 competitor who dressed as Captain Kidd—and finished last. Many have followed where this buccaneer led, transforming it into an athletic-themed Mardi Gras. When I ran it recently, I had some conspicuously fit men dressed as mermaids near me at the start. One mermaid worried aloud about getting into an exclusive post-run party, and his friend scoffed, "Dude, we're mermaids. We're getting in."

My running companion and I lost the quick-stepping mermaids on the Hayes Street Hill, but there were still some good costumes nearby. At the hilltop, I saw an octet of roller-skaters in sequin-spangled purple bodysuits, dressed to look like the pop singer Prince, who had just died. In the year David Bowie died, I also saw three runners impersonating him in his Ziggy Stardust period, lightning bolts across their faces, red hair bolt upright.

One group, though, does not vary its costume from year to year. They dress as salmon and run against the race's flow, swimming upstream. This contrariness seems very San Francisco—as do those runners who dress in nothing but their sneakers.

For many years, as at a Mardi Gras celebration, the booze flowed freely during Bay to Breakers, with open house parties lining the route. Some blamed the alcohol, in part, for two deaths—one a spectator who fell from a rooftop party, the other killed in a brawl between a group dressed as trolls and another in 49ers gear. Whether it's been the crackdowns by organizers or the rise of a new, more abstemious generation, there's been markedly less drunk and disorderly behavior at Bay to Breakers lately.

For me, Bay to Breakers becomes more race than fiesta at a certain point. When, in Golden Gate Park, I get the first whiff of salty ocean air, my competitive juices start to flow. I start to think I'll be damned if I'm finishing after that coastal redwood—think how much extra weight he's got to lug with that 6-foot model tree on his shoulders. Those two brides up ahead are flagging—if I bear down, maybe I can catch them. But, beware, that eggplant behind is coming on.

Bay to Breakers presents lots of surreal sights and outdoes itself right near the end, when runners of this ever-so-urban race find there are buffalo grazing to the right.

Bison have made their home on various ranges of Golden Gate Park since 1890, when keepers acquired a cow (named for actress Sarah Bernhardt) and a bull (Ben Harrison, for the then president). The park has long run a breeding program, with at least 100 calves born here and many heading out to join their peers in less urban zip codes. The park's small herd, all female, occupy a paddock on the race route (1237 John F. Kennedy Dr.). They are descended not from Ben and Sarah, but from an unusual birthday gift. In 1984, investment banker Richard Blum gave a pair of buffalo to his wife, Dianne Feinstein. The city's former mayor, later a senator, decided not to keep them in her own backyard.

Civic Center & The Tenderloin

5,000–3,000 BC

OLDEST ART ON DISPLAY

MUSHROOM BOTTLE AT THE ASIAN ART MUSEUM CHONG-MOON LEE CENTER FOR ASIAN ART AND CULTURE

200 Larkin St.

The longtime director of the Asian Art Museum, Jay Xu, has been known to attend staff meetings as a medieval samurai, bearing an antique sword. "Just for fun, to motivate staff," he says.

The largest American museum devoted to Asian art has, under Xu, moved into the major leagues of international institutions. But its business is still, in large part, to show off many small things to maximum effect. For instance, the oldest piece in the collection and the oldest artifact on display in San Francisco is a wee mushroom-shaped jar from the stone-age culture that lived on the banks of Huang He River (aka the Yellow River) between 5,000 and 7,000 years ago. Much of what we know of this culture comes out of a big find in 1952, at the so-called Banpo site. In this perennially flood-plagued region, the people tended to live in settlements surrounded by moats, with kilns at the edges where they made both functional pottery and more ornamental pieces, like the jar. Its mushroom shape features the red and black decoration of the period. "The patterns might represent mountains and waves," a museum rep says. "It's too small for a drinking vessel for water, and it probably stored some important liquid or valuable powder, something with a special ritual or medical use." Ritual obviously played a part in this subsistence culture, with some artisans producing bigger pottery jars in which dead babies were buried, others using silk for some special garments.

"It is from this area that the Chinese civilization grew," Xu says.

As I wandered the museum to find the jar, I was also taken by the screen painted in 19th-century Korea with a scholar's core needs on it (books and pens); the jade sculptures backlit to reveal their luminescence; the colorful stick puppets from Java; and the tiny netsuke, many carved in animal shapes, worn by Japanese men, attached to kimono sashes.

For his part, Xu enthuses over the museum's famous Korean moon jar. "It's a little asymmetrical, and we've displayed it off center in its case, on some partially finished wood—the beauty of imperfection is part of what it is about."

All this resides in a building full of drama—a central staircase with light streaming down from skylights and a lofty great hall that was once the centerpiece of the main civic library. The Beaux-Arts structure was designed by architect George Kelham and completed in 1917. The job of morphing it into a museum fell to Gae Aulenti, the architect who changed a Parisian train station into the Musée D'Orsay. Her conversion was deft, supplementing the building with glassed-in atriums supported by celadon-green beams between the three wings.

"We want to bring Asian arts and culture to the East Coast of the Pacific," says Xu. In samurai costume and out, he's been motivating his staff

Courtesy Asian Art Museum of San Francisco

to curate exhibits that address Asian cultures in their own terms—and to feature the work of contemporary Asian-American and Asian artists.

Part of the museum's great financial leap forward is due to Asian-American donors. The museum was renamed for Korean-American media baron Chong-Moon Lee after a $15-million contribution in 1995, and the lead contribution of $25 million for the recent renovation was made by Yahoo cofounder Jerry Yang and wife Akiko Yamazaki.

Does Xu worry about frosty relations between the US and China? "It is always important to understand other cultures, to try to transcend the present moment."

The long view is certainly encouraged when contemplating a little vase made about 7,000 years ago for reasons unknown in a small village next to a great river.

Completed in 1994, the new main branch of the San Francisco Public Library (100 Larkin St.) sits next to the old one, now the Asian's home. It has twice as much space as the old library did, with one wall filled with an artwork made of remainders from the institution's now-digitized card catalog. And, though large, it houses many small and congenial special collections: the San Francisco History Room, the Wallace E. Stegner Environmental Center, and the Steve Silver Beach Blanket Babylon Music Center—the latter named for a long-running campy local theatrical and its producer. The Library also has its own social worker to refer clients to support they might need, and was one of the first in the nation to stop charging late fines and forgive old ones.

1923

OLDEST OPERA COMPANY

SAN FRANCISCO OPERA

301 Van Ness Ave.

"Strong, opinionated, devious, affectionate, elegant, caring, vindictive, argumentative, ruthless." These are among the adjectives that American soprano Leontyne Price once used to describe the man who brought her to the San Francisco Opera. The company's second head, Kurt Herbert Adler, cast her in the North American premiere of *Dialogues of the Carmelites* in 1957. In that season, Price would go on to sub for an ailing diva in *Aida*, an opera whose lead she would own for years.

"I didn't have time be sweet and nice," Adler once admitted. Even so, more than any other individual, he put the city on the operatic map, where it stays to this day. A company with a nearly $80-million budget, it recently celebrated, with all due pageantry, its centennial.

The company planted itself in fertile ground: Touring operas drew enthusiastic crowds in San Francisco from the Gold Rush on. By one historian's count, some 5,000 operas were performed in 26 different local theaters from the 1850s to the 1906 earthquake. Famously, tenor Enrico Caruso was here when the quake hit (staying in the Palace Hotel) and fled the city afterwards, vowing never to come back.

Another Italian opera artist, the Neapolitan conductor Gaetano Merola, later came on tour to the city and stayed, hoping to build a company. After bringing some singers to perform at Stanford's football stadium in 1922, Merola established the company as a

Courtesy San Francisco Opera

leading purveyor of classical opera. In 1932, architect Arthur Brown Jr. gave it an acoustically impressive house that went on to achieve some nonmusical distinctions. In 1949 the United Nations Charter was signed, and in 1951 the sovereignty of Japan was officially restored, in the building.

In 1953 Merola died of a heart attack midway through conducting an outdoor performance of an aria from *Madame Butterfly*. His longtime chorus master, Adler, rushed to his side—and soon firmly took the company's reins in his hands, not relinquishing them until the 1980s.

Today, arts administrator Matthew Shivlock serves as its General Director, while Korean conductor Eun Sun Kim is its Music Director.

Big stars continue to feel at ease here, with Luciano Pavarotti calling it his second home and Placido Domingo flying in from New York to sub in for a sick leading man in *Otello*. The company has also brought along young talent, nurturing the likes of Anna Netrebko and Deborah Voigt, and championed some important new operas—among them works by Bay Area–based composers John Adams and Jake Heggie.

But the art has never been the only thing going on. From 1941 on, the Opera Ball that opened the fall season became a must-attend for San Francisco society, the street theatre of the patrons' arrival often every bit as dramatic as what would be staged. In her book *Dancing on the Brink of the World*, former society columnist Frances Moffat writes of the intergenerational turf wars fought here between members of the so-called Golden Circle—what counted as Old Money back in the day—and the Jet Set of the 1960s and '70s.

At one year's ball, Moffat clocked a topaz tiara, once belonging to French Empress Eugenie, worn by Mrs. Milton Esberg Jr., while sugar heiress Dorothy Spreckels rocked a $15,000 platinum mink coat. At another gala, when presidential spouse Lady Bird Johnson was the guest of honor, Moffat reported on the anti-Vietnam protesters outside the building as well as the fight within, between society women trying to get featured in the next day's paper.

More recently, the first post-COVID ball had Banana Republic President Jack Calhoun, resplendent in a gold brocade tuxedo, hobnobbing with philanthropist Dede Wilsey, clad in a green metallic sheath.

The country's oldest professional dance troupe, the San Francisco Ballet (455 Franklin St.) performs its main season at the opera house. Founded in 1933, the company has toured around the world and achieved international distinction.

Three Danish American brothers helped put the company en pointe. Early artistic director Willam Christensen programmed the first full-length North American productions of Swan Lake *and* The Nutcracker. *The 1944 production of the latter on Christmas Eve helped launch the tradition of putting it on at holiday time in cities around the continent. Brother Harold Christensen would run the school in its early years, while the other brother Lew after training with modernist choreographer George Balanchine in New York, succeeded Willam as company head. Another Balanchine disciple, Helgi Tómasson, would lead the company from 1985 on, only recently announcing his retirement. The influence of Balanchine's clean, unfussy aesthetic is evident here.*

1969

OLDEST RECORDING STUDIO

HYDE STREET STUDIOS

245 Hyde St.

Through these doors have walked many of the great music-makers of the past half-century. Here Creedence Clearwater Revival warned about a bad moon rising; Crosby, Stills, Nash & Young told parents to teach their children well; and Grace Slick asked, emphatically, "Don't you want somebody love?"

Growing up in Oregon, the studio's founder Wally Heider always loved music, but his sax playing was poor enough that once a band leader asked him to turn his instrument away from the microphone. And so he went to law school and worked for a few years as an attorney. But the music wouldn't let him be, so the tall, stutter-prone man apprenticed at a big LA studio (the one where the Beach Boys recorded *Pet Sounds*), becoming a specialist in mobile recording.

Heider was one of those who captured the epochal Monterey Pop Festival in 1967—and is shown in film reels of the event rushing onstage to rescue some valuable microphones from The Who's Pete Townsend and Keith Moon, who were intent on

trashing them with their guitars. Many of the stars who emerged at that festival became friends with Heider, and when he started this studio, they came, they played, they conquered, creating the so-called San Francisco Sound. The big studios elsewhere tended to have regimented schedules, and lots of rules—no touching the master board, no using the echo chamber after five.

Here, really, anything went. David Crosby entertained girlfriends upstairs while Slick passed out on a couch, her double-parked Aston Martin accruing parking tickets outside. Yet despite this freedom, the hits kept on coming. If Carlos Santana wanted the studio lit in red to get him in the right place to serve up a guitar riff, it would be done.

Heider retired in the late '70s, selling what is now, under owner Michael Ward, the oldest remaining multi-studio set-up in the city. Even with Heider gone, though, the beat didn't stop. Here, the Dead Kennedys recorded legendary punk squawks, rapper Tupac did his first solo album, and contemporary artists as diverse as Green Day, Rufus Wainwright, and Cake followed where the Grateful Dead, the Byrds, and Van Morrison long ago led.

In the hallways the walls are awash in gold and platinum records—one for Train's "Hey, Soul Sister" says it sold 6,000,000. "The album covers, they're a history of design over the last half century, aren't they?" studio manager Jack Kertzman says. On a bookcase there's a pamphlet titled, "How to Make Your Band Sound Good."

"We have a new platinum record poster coming, OneRepublic's 'Rescue Me'", he adds, as he consults with the groups and individuals using different studios, a sax blowing when he opens one door, some acoustic guitar licks when he peers into another studio. An intern says the soundproofing is good enough that the weekend before, a drummer was rocking out in one studio and didn't bother an author doing a recording of a book in the one below.

With the Bay Area's housing prices, how do the artists manage to live here? Kertzman says, "Everyone does their best. What they write about how the scene is dead, all the creatives are gone . . . it's not dead. I live in North Beach and I can listen to live music, if I want to, every night."

He says he loves to watch, from his perch behind the sound board, an entire album take shape. "When you're here for a whole stretch of days—especially the instrumentation coming together, that's what's exciting. I just got to do that with these young guys from the East Coast, the Lemon Twigs, cool music, insanely talented. It was exactly why I went into this."

When Crosby, Stills, Nash & Young were recording their album Déjà Vu *on Hyde Street, Neil Young stayed nearby at a motel called The Caravan. It was an unlikely property to find in the Tenderloin, done in Mid-century Modern style, with a courtyard in the middle and a kidney-shaped pool. In the 1970s and '80s, the place fell on hard times until would-be hotelier Chip Conley bought it, pimped it up, and turned it into The Phoenix (601 Eddy St.). Since then, it's played host to the likes of David Bowie, the Red Hot Chili Peppers, and Pearl Jam. Once, Debbie Harry and John F. Kennedy Jr. accidentally checked into the same room. A note scrawled on Phoenix stationery was found in the pocket of Kurt Cobain after his suicide, and his partner Courtney Love reputedly skinny-dipped in the Palm Springs–worthy pool. The pool is now a registered as a national landmark.*

NORTH OF DOWNTOWN

NORTH BEACH, ALCATRAZ ISLAND, FISHERMAN'S WHARF, RUSSIAN HILL, PACIFIC HEIGHTS, THE MARINA

1879

OLDEST JEANS

LEVI STRAUSS & CO.

1155 Battery St.

The legend is this: Merchant Levi Strauss sailed to San Francisco and, on arrival, took down his abandoned ship's sails and began to make pants. "A lovely, romantic story," says Tracey Panek, the in-house historian at the company that bears his name. "But it's just not true." The tale came into being, perhaps, because some of the prospectors who came to San Francisco did repurpose the sails of their ships into tents as they panned for gold up in the Sierras.

In fact, Strauss was a storekeeper who came to New York from Buttenheim, Bavaria, in 1846 and joined a dry-goods shop founded by his brothers. In 1853 he came to booming San Francisco to set up a branch that supplied, among many other things, tough cotton for work-pants.

Courtesy Levi Strauss & Co. Archives

Then Jacob Davis, a Nevada tailor, came up with the concept of putting steel rivets at the trousers' stress points to make them last longer. "A working man's wife came to him," Panek says, "and complained that she couldn't keep her husband in pants. Davis was working on a horse blanket at the same time, which had some steel elements, clips." The riveted pants proved so popular that soon he couldn't keep up with the demand, and he wrote to his San Francisco supplier proposing a partnership. In 1873 the pair took out US Patent No. 139,121, and Strauss started making the pants we now call Levi's.

From a fireproof safe at the conglomerate's headquarters, Panek removes the oldest known pair of jeans, and I feel I'm getting a private viewing of the Shroud of Turin. This pair has buttons in the waist for suspenders and a tiny slot for a pocket-watch. The oldest pair is faded, of course it is, with multiple stretches at the knee—"several people probably wore them. One of them, we think, a miner."

Panek speaks of the brand's changing clientele over time. The female riveters who helped in the shipbuilding plants around the San Francisco Bay during WWII often wore Levi's. "I spoke to one of these women called the Rosies, who wore them to keep the sparks from hitting her legs." After the war, according to Panek, some soldiers wanted to preserve the sense of the brotherhood they'd felt over there, so they started up motorcycle clubs (the Hell's Angels in Oakland was among them), wearing—what else?—Levi's. With assists from on-screen rebels like Marlon Brando and James Dean, the pants developed an antiestablishment chic, confirmed when some schools banned them in the 1950s.

Panek attributes a 1960's design innovation to a woman who operated a boutique in the Haight. "She was friends with Janis Joplin, Jimi Hendrix. She started to see people walking by her store who'd added some fabric at the bottom of their pants. She asked someone in to show her how to do it, starting making them, and they soon became very popular." She approached the company, and they collaborated with her to make the quintessential bit of outdoor concert gear, the bellbottom.

In the 1980s, AIDS hit San Francisco's gay community hard. "I moved here then," Panek says, "and many people were afraid to visit the city, afraid they'd get it in a restaurant." In the thick of the pandemic, some employees proposed to distribute pamphlets to staff with the best information they had. "The man who became our CEO decided to share the information himself, so that the employees didn't get stigmatized," says Panek. Still run by relatives of Strauss, the company also became the first big corporate donor to help fund an AIDS clinic in the city.

Just around the corner from Levi's corporate headquarters is the former workshop (202 Green St.) of another man who took out a famous patent. A Mormon farm-boy with a knack for making his family ranch's generator go, Philo T. Farnsworth helped develop one of the world's first televisions in 1928. In a moment reminiscent of Alexander Graham Bell's first telephone call, he successfully transmitted encoded images from one room to another, announcing, "There you are—electronic television." Farnsworth also pioneered devices to aid in the detection of submarines and to help in air-traffic control, logging a total of about 300 patents in his lifetime. But he didn't make as much from his patent for the electronic television as did Strauss from the one for riveted work pants. Prolonged legal disputes with RCA drained his bank account—though he did win most of them. He died, in 1971, with not much to show for his ingenuity.

1953

OLDEST PAPERBACK BOOKSTORE

CITY LIGHTS

261 Columbus Ave.

It's no "Dr. Livingston, I presume," but there is something to this meeting, something sweet and geeky. The young artist Lawrence Ferlinghetti was walking home from his Mission Street studio toward his home in North Beach. On Columbus he ran into someone he'd heard about, Peter Martin, the editor of a magazine called *City Lights*. The son of a famous anarchist, Martin had decided to expand from producing a magazine into books, and he was putting his imprint's "Pocket Books" sign on the street. When Ferlinghetti introduced himself, Martin said, "Oh, you're the one who sent me [some French] translations."

Ferlinghetti would later write: "It was Peter Martin's brilliant idea to have the first all-paperbound bookstore in the country." Before the midcentury, paperbacks were mainly pulpy bodice-rippers, sold in spinners at drugstores and bus stations. But across the Atlantic, Penguin was starting to release great literature in soft covers, and American publishers were beginning to follow suit. With an investment of $500 each, Ferlinghetti and Martin soon set up their shop in a part of this triangular building, giving it the name of Martin's magazine. (The magazine had the signal distinction of publishing Pauline Kael on film, years before she'd start writing on the same subject for *The New Yorker*.)

The shop is located in a building named for two French brothers, Émile and Jean Artigues—and that's somehow appropriate. Frenchness was in City Lights's DNA, from the kiosks of used books out front to its highbrow love of avant-garde art movements (there's a Surrealism shelf), to the slightly look-at-me leftism in its mix (nonfiction downstairs is filed on shelves labeled Muckraking, Class War, and Stolen Continents). Like Shakespeare & Co., the bookstore started in Paris by a friend of Ferlinghetti's, City Lights has become a global mecca for readers, a hang-out spot where you can read all day with no staff throat-clearing nearby.

I was one of those who made a pilgrimage here in my first trip to San Francisco in 1987, since it had published that primal scream of a poem, Allen Ginsberg's *Howl* in 1955, and since it was the place to which Jack Kerouac sent postcards when he was on the road, writing the book of that name. I bought both, of course. There were other books there to open up the mind: Howard Zinn's *People's History of the US*, Armistead Maupin's early installments of *Tales of the City*, Denise Levertov's 1957 poetry volume *Here and Now*, less celebrated than her contemporary Ginsberg's work, but equally vivid. By then Peter Martin had long returned to his native New York, and the store had begun to carry hardbacks.

Luckily, Ferlinghetti and longtime store staffer and former head of the publishing house Nancy Peters were able to buy the building in 2000, as rents in tech-era San Francisco began to spike. No longer can many young, aspiring poet-painters cover the rent on a crash-pad in North Beach and a studio on Mission Street. At the grand old age of 101, Ferlinghetti died in February 2021, leaving behind him a threefold legacy, the shop, the publishing house, and his defense, long ago, of literature's prerogatives to turn on and offend. To shoppers in the store, he has addressed a hand-lettered sign, one with a politically motivated word tweak: "Stash your Sell Phone and Be Here Now."

A couple of blocks away from City Lights is Caffe Trieste (601 Vallejo St.), also a former Beat hangout, still a magnet for Bohemians and Characters with a capital 'C'. Founded in 1956 by immigrants from that Northern Italian city, it advertises itself as the first espresso house on the West Coast. All of the Giotta family are musicians, with photos lining the walls of Papa Gianni, Mamma Ida, and their children Gianfranco, Sonia, and Fabio giving their all. In addition to the weekly musical concert, Trieste often hosts literary readings. Its website conveys the mix on offer here: "Old Italy, Bohemian poets, art and music, and excellent espresso." There's often an accordionist playing at Trieste; the eavesdropping is peerless. When asked about his success, Papa Gianni would say, "No big deal. Buy the best beans, roast them yourself and brew each cup like it's for you."

1911–1912

OLDEST COMMERCIAL OVEN

LIGURIA BAKERY

1700 Stockton St.

There are fancier food pleasures in this multiple Michelin-starred city, but getting a focaccia still hot from Liguria's oven, taking it to a bench across the way in Washington Square, and devouring it—that has to rank right up there.

Members of the Soracco family have been producing bread daily on the corner of Stockton and Filbert for over a century. At first they produced loaves, bread sticks, and buns, but as bigger, more corporate bakeries began to make incursions, the Soraccos focused mainly on focaccia, the famous dimpled flatbread of the Northern Italian region from whence they came, Liguria.

It was shortly after the San Francisco quake of 1906 that the first owner, Ambrogio Soracco, arrived from that region's largest city, Genoa, and Washington Square still had tents full of refugees camped out on it. He worked in other neighborhood bakeries, making loaves for many of the approximately 17,000 Italian immigrants to arrive in the city in that period.

Ambrogio died in the late '30s, while his son George was still a boy, leaving his mother to manage things, with the help of some longtime bakers, at least until he graduated from high school. George began running the bakery in 1947 and didn't stop until he died, at age 84, in 2013. Says his son, Michael, who's carried on the business, "It was his life. He worked 18 hours a day, for 66 years, Christmas, New Year's, all the time."

The highly physical work begins in the wee hours of the morning, usually at around 3:00 a.m., and involves a mechanical mixer that's only a little less ancient than the oven, also over a century old. The dough is made from flour still purchased from the original supplier. After the mixing, the dough gets three separate proofs before it goes in this trusty old oven. The pans of foccacia start to come out of the 700-degree oven just before the bakery opens, at 7:00 a.m. There's often a line then, and the focaccia loaves (at $8 a pop) are usually snapped up by 10 a.m.

A constellation of relatives has worked here over the years, Michael's sister and mother running the counter for a time, wrapping the loaves carefully in string and butcher paper, his daughter and nephew sometimes helping out in more recent years. Many of them are shown in photos on the walls. But mainly it's been a business built and carried on by three generations of Soracco men. Michael (known as Mikey to intimates) began baking there in 1981. "To work with your father for as long as I did, almost every day for 32 years, it was this amazing thing. And now for him not to be there, it's a hole."

Although he no longer works on Christmas, the in-house panettone produced in the run-up to the holidays is first-rate—and also sells out quickly. But the main draw here is the focaccia, which comes with several toppings. The most popular has pizza sauce and cheese on it, but my favorite is the one topped with rosemary. As for Michael, he likes the plain, unadulterated loaves.

In Liguria's window are some old scales, a pre-electric cash register, and some wooden paddles, scorched from putting loaves in, and taking them out of the old oven. Above them is a sign bearing the bakery's telephone number from way back, "Garfield 13786." Though Liguria now has a modern 415-area-code number, it still has no website and does no advertising. "The bread," Michael says, "it has to be its own advertisement."

The Soraccos' family church, Saints Peter and Paul (666 Filbert St.) also faces onto Washington Square. Founded by Italian immigrants in 1884, the original building was destroyed in the aftermath of the quake. The new Santi Pietro e Paolo—its name sounds better in Italian—is made of white marble and was finished in 1924. (Local poet Lawrence Ferlinghetti once called it the "marzipan church.") A few years after its completion, the church was besieged by anti-Catholic anarchists, a campaign that ended with police killing two of the would-be bombers on the church steps, one of them with dynamite in his hands.

A happier story involves baseball legend Joe DiMaggio. After growing up in the neighborhood, he got married here, in 1939, to his first wife Dorothy Arnold, and had pictures taken on its steps after his City Hall marriage in 1954 to Marilyn Monroe. In "Mrs. Robinson," Simon & Garfunkel asked plaintively, "Where have you gone, Joe DiMaggio?" and it was here, at the last, that his body came, for his 1999 funeral.

1873

OLDEST ROWING AND SWIM CLUB

SOUTH END ROWING CLUB

500 Jefferson St.

The South End Rowing Club occupies a site at the northern tip of the San Francisco peninsula—which makes a certain kind of San Francisco sense. After all, not far from this old club, there's a square named for George Washington with a statue in its center of . . . Benjamin Franklin. Though San Francisco loves to confound expectations, the South End once had a solid claim to this name: It started its life on the edge of what was then Mission Bay, a body of water south of the city center, now largely filled in. That bay once harbored ships that were loaded and offloaded by boats rowed by watermen, some of them among the club's first members.

Rowing was all the rage in the city's early years, and the club often competed against its fierce rivals, the Ariels (founded a little earlier) and Dolphins (later). The Southenders were the victors in an overnight race in 1927 from San Francisco to Stockton, just over 60 miles of rowing in two-person skiffs—an event later dubbed the Amazing Race. There were triumphs, for sure, but also some tragedies in the club's early years, as when five teenagers broke into the club in 1908, borrowed some boats, and drowned in the Bay.

In the 20th century, in America at least, rowing has acquired an upper-class patina, supposedly favored by square-jawed, long-limbed Ivy Leaguers. But in the South End's early days, the sport was popular among the working class, the watermen, stevedores, boat-builders, and their drinking buddies. The club's early rolls included machinists, clerks and a tavern owner, tinsmiths, blacksmiths and butchers—and "not a single member of the professions, nary a lawyer or a doctor or teacher, and just one lonely reporter," according to Bob Barde, who wrote a history of the club with an assist from Pat Cunneen. Its members were also, mainly, of Irish extraction, and since 1928 the club has hosted an annual St. Patrick's Day party.

"The working class feel, the Irish influence, those are still with us," says current president Fran Hegeler, director of marketing and communications at a landscape architecture firm. If that hasn't changed, something else has, since Hegeler is the third female president of the longtime male bastion. She was elected by

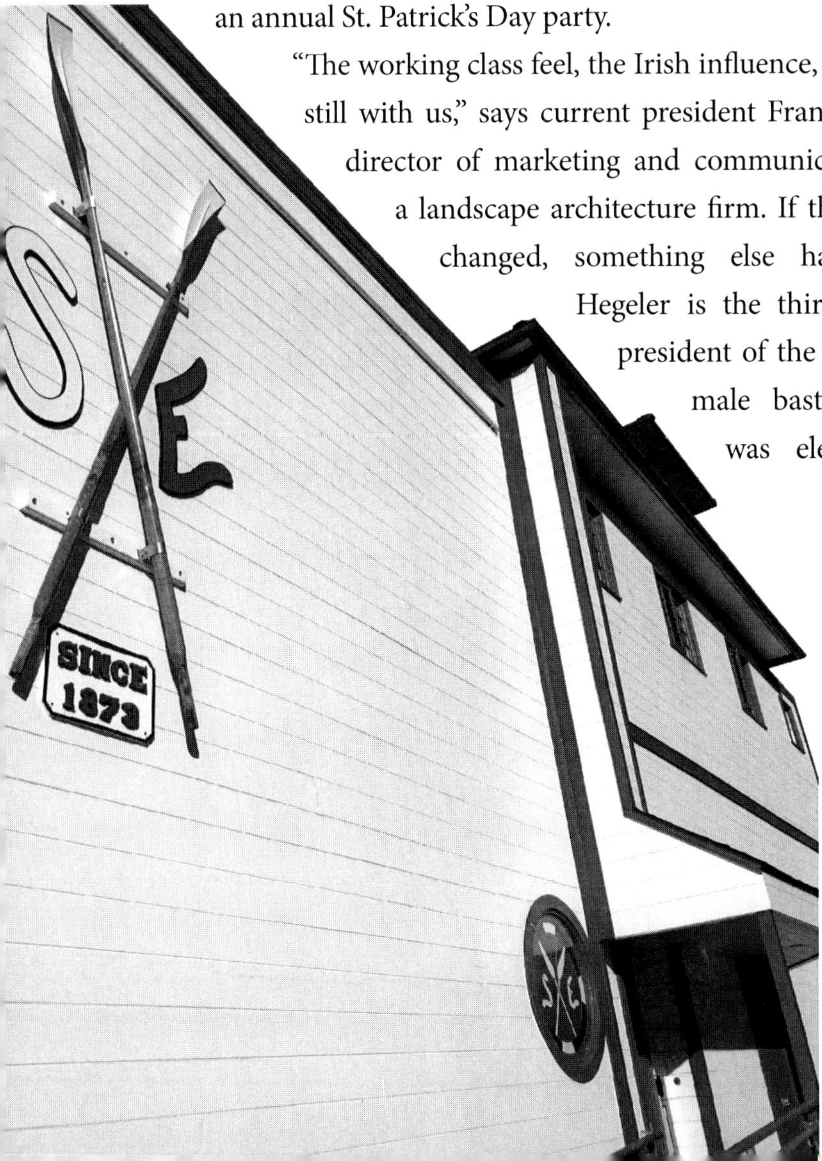

a membership of about 900, two-thirds of them men, one-third women. “That change, from men-only, to let women in, that didn’t come easily, but the guys are now on side, big supporters.”

Two other big changes also came to the South End: Though the club remains a rowing club, its members now also enjoy swimming and handball—a 13-time national handball champion, Rudy (The Dominator) Stadlberger played from here. Rowing is still done, in a mix of lovingly preserved old wooden boats and state-of-the-art modern skiffs, but most of the membership is focused on braving the frigid Bay waters during all four seasons.

What are the challenges of swimming in the Bay? “You have some critter contact sometimes,” Hegeler says. “The sharks mainly ignore you, and the harbor seals are cute, but sometimes something brushes you.” One of the members supposedly punched a sea-lion in the nose in the last few years to force it to back off. “But that feeling, when you get in, when you’re in, you feel exhilarated, alive, completely in your body.” (I’ve done it once, with a member of its next-door rival, the Dolphin Club, and “exhilarating” is certainly one word for it—once your pulse settles and your heart stops pounding at the shock of entry.)

“When you get back from a long swim,” Hegeler says, “you never value a hot shower more.”

1849

OLDEST BAKERY

BOUDIN

160 Jefferson St., with other locations around the city

Courtesy Boudin Bakery

The subtitle of the Boudin Bakery's story should be The Virtue of Stubbornness. Founded in the thick of the Gold Rush by one of the sudden city's many French immigrants, Isidore Boudin, the bakery has carried on doing its one main thing, its distinctive sourdough bread, through the better part of two centuries.

There are some overlapping tales about the bread's starter. It is rumored to have been passed to Boudin by a gold prospector, a '49er, but also to have come with Isidore from France. It is certainly enriched with an airborne yeast that seems characteristic of this city—so much so that it has been saddled with the mouthful Latin handle of *lactobacillus sanfranciscensis.*

Boudin had a ready-made, French-style bread market here, since, as of 1852, nearly one in six of the 36,000 San Franciscans came from France, many of them escaping turmoil and widespread unemployment in the mother country. Soon enough, the horse-drawn Boudin bread-wagon became a familiar sight on the hilly streets, its delivery-men pushing the distinctively scored, rounded loaves onto nails regular customers left protruding next to their doors.

In the 1860s a reliable commercial yeast pioneered by Fleischmann's became all the rage among bakeries. But Boudin declined to use it in the first display of the stubbornness that would become (sorry) baked into the company's DNA.

In 1873, the by-then prosperous Isidore married another French ex-pat, Louise Erni, who has a central role in the Boudin story. She kept her head in the 1906 quake, rescuing the sourdough starter in a bucket as she fled the bakery's soon-to-be-destroyed premises.

In 1935, Boudin's descendants had the good sense to hire an Italian named Stefano Giraudo, perhaps comforting themselves at the time with the knowledge that he'd trained in a French bakery in Toulon. For 60 years, Papa Steve (as he became known in-house) was Boudin's early-to-rise master baker. He purchased Boudin in 1941; by then, its pronunciation had been thoroughly Americanized to 'boo-deen'. His grandson Daniel Giraudo is part of the current ownership team.

In the 1960s many older bakeries began to adopt a new generation of fast-acting, low-cost yeasts, but again Boudin declined. "We've stuck to our process," Daniel says of their labor-intensive, three-day method. "We've never tried to be someone that we're not."

In 1993, the family sold the company to a midwestern bakery-chain owner Specialty Foods, which took some steps to homogenize Boudin's offerings—even while it held onto the mother-dough starter and kept on Fernando Padilla, Papa Steve's successor as master baker.

In part because of his close relationship with his grandfather, Daniel (and business partner Sharon Duvall) bought Boudin back in 2002. This meant that Papa Steve got to see his legacy back in family hands before dying in 2012—at the French Hospital, another institution built by early emigrants from France. Daniel has put Papa Steve's photo in all of Boudin's nearly 30 branches.

Sourdough went out of fashion for a while. But it's roared back recently, with many other Bay Area bakeries, the likes of Acme and Semifreddi's, churning out tangy loaves that are fermented with the help of airborne yeast. "Our competitors have come around to our methods. I don't see that as a negative," Daniel says, before going into sales mode. "There's a renewed appreciation of the romance around the sourdough, the fermentation. Also, fermented products are better for you."

The store's flagship bakery has an industrial fridge with a sign saying, "The Mother Dough lives here"—a tribute to Boudin's stubborn allegiance, over nearly 175 years, to the starter that helped it get going.

A good finish to a long bread-and-seafood lunch at the Boudin bistro can be had nearby at the historic Buena Vista Café (2765 Hyde St.). It has the signal distinction of having introduced the Irish Coffee to America on November 10, 1952.

This legendary mixture of coffee, Irish whiskey, sugar, and cream arrived here courtesy of Stanton Delaplane, a San Francisco Chronicle *writer. He'd tasted the concoction at the Shannon Airport and worked with his friend, the Buena Vista's owner Jack Koeppler, to recreate it. The city's mayor, George Christopher, who'd worked in dairy, recommended they age the cream for at least two days to maximize the float.*

The bar tends to go from festive to positively raucous on the anniversary of the drink's American debut. A recent celebration featured an effort to get into the Guinness Book of World Records *with the largest Irish Coffee ever. Troupes of clog-dancers and bagpipers have also been known to participate.*

1886

OLDEST SHIP

BALCLUTHA

San Francisco Maritime National Historic Park, 2 Marina Blvd.

Various survivors of the overlapping Ages of Sail and Steam line the Hyde Street Pier, a collection of vintage tugs, ferries, and schooners. The oldest, and perhaps the one with the most checkered history, is the *Balclutha*, a three-masted ship just over 250 feet long, built in Scotland. In Gaelic, its name means, roughly, a Town on the River Clyde, and it was a busy shipyard in a town downriver from Glasgow that produced the steel-hulled, 1,862-ton windjammer.

The *Balclutha* began its life as a merchant ship, bringing to California coal and manufactured items, taking grain back to industrialized, bread-hungry Europe. Twice the ship almost met its end, once nearly colliding with a sea-going tornado off Cape Horn, another time foundering on a reef in the Bristol Channel, the pigs on-board getting washed away. But, soon the boat was righted and readied to sail again.

The Park Ranger–led tours give some feel for what the long voyages aboard must have been like—it could take about 140 days to get from Europe to the West Coast. From the elevated poop deck at the stern of the boat officers could see much of what going on onboard. There's a wooden helm right out of *Master and Commander* there, now mainly used for photo opportunities.

Below deck, the staterooms for the captain and his mates have some elegance to them. The so-called saloon, mainly original, is paneled with yellow pine and trimmed with teak, oak, mahogany, and bird's-eye maple. A bar is attached to the ceiling by hinges so that no matter how much the ship listed, its bottles were kept level.

Made at the tail end of the Age of Sail, the ship increasingly couldn't keep pace with its many mechanized competitors. In 1906 it was sold to the Alaska Packers' Association to carry fishermen and cannery workers up the coast to Alaska for the spring and bring them back with thousands of tins of fish.

Towards the end of the 1920s, the ship again foundered on a reef and was sold for $500 as she lay. A few years later the *Balclutha* fell into the hands of a rakish former carnival performer by the name of Tex Kissinger. He felt certain the ship could help him realize various money-making ventures, each more cockamamie than the last.

First, there was the idea of making it a floating zoo, exhibiting vampire bats and stingrays, boa constrictors and giant turtles. Nothing came of it. Then, with a crew of adventure-seeking teenaged boys, it headed to a barrier island off Mexico to capture elephant seals to sell to actual zoos. Kissinger and crew realized they didn't know at all what they were doing when an irritated bull elephant charged at them. The tail end of a hurricane then hit the ship and the boys' mothers went into a frenzy, going as high as the US President in their petitions to repatriate the *Balclutha*.

Moored for years near Los Angeles, the ship had better luck as an extra in various films before coming back to San Francisco for the 1939 World's Fair, where it hosted a louche set of exhibits about pirates and torture.

One of the Maritime Museum's founders, Karl Kortum, made it his life's mission to buy and restore ships that evoke the romance of a bygone era. After prolonged dickering with Kissinger's widow, he and his board got a hold of the *Balclutha*, convincing a host of dock-workers to restore it to some of its former glory. Since then the museum's team has built, ship by ship, a small fleet here.

While the Balclutha *was crossing the oceans, the oldest extant ferry, the* Eureka, *completed in 1890, was carrying passengers and railcars that arrived in Marin County across the Golden Gate strait. After WWI the steam-driven ferry was gutted and converted to enable it to carry those newfangled conveyances, automobiles.*

Another dock-mate is the only remaining ocean-going steam tug on the West Coast, the Hercules, *built in 1907. Back in the day, the doughty tug towed ships into Pearl Harbor and helped equip the Panama Canal with the machinery used to open and close the locks.*

At the other end of Aquatic Park, in the Maritime Museum's building, is the Mermaid, *a 19-foot plywood sloop, piloted solo by 23-year-old Kenichi Horie from Osaka to San Francisco in 1962. He was arrested when he entered the Golden Gate, but then, when the extent of his achievement became known, he received the key to the city.*

1947

OLDEST NONPROFIT SENIOR CENTER

SAN FRANCISCO SENIOR CENTER

890 Beach St., 481 O'Farrell St.

The first nonprofit center for seniors in the city—also the first in the nation—got going thanks to Charles Rose. We know but little about him. A retiree, he lived in a sort of dwelling that is relatively common in the core of San Francisco, a single-room-occupancy hotel, not far from Union Square. On sunny days he and his cronies would hang out on the square, but when it rained they'd be shut in their small pads with just the radio for company. Sick of the isolation, he and his chums marched down to City Hall and pushed, it seems, the right buttons—an administrator found some space for them. Overlooking the Golden Gate strait, the Aquatic Park Bathhouse looks like a beached ocean liner. The Moderne-style building was put up by the federal Works Progress Administration and the city in 1939. During WWII the army commandeered it, vacating it afterwards. Part became the Maritime Museum, the other an indoor gathering spot for Rose and other seniors.

The Center was soon taken over by a social worker whom many regard as a visionary, Margaret Vickery, who helped to found the field of gerontology and ran the center for its first 20 years. Her core insight is that seniors must plan and lead the group activities as well as participating in them. She writes in *How to Work with Older People*: "We must decide whether the program in our community

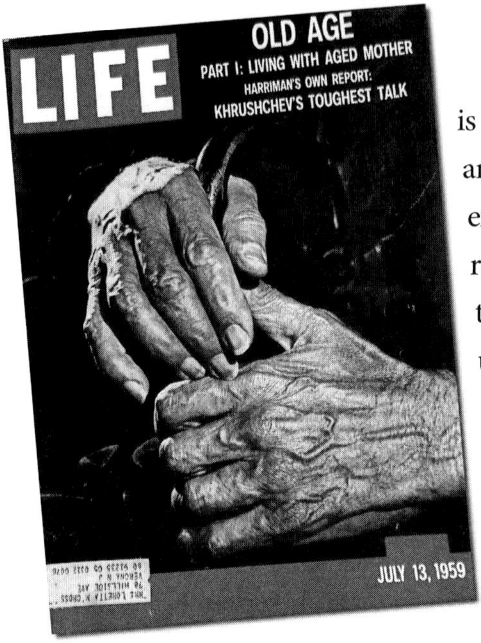

is to become an island of isolation and escape, offering pleasant experiences to older people without responsibility, and thus increase the feelings of despondency and uselessness."

One of Vickery's successors was Sue Horst, who headed the center from 2012 until 2020. "Vickery was way ahead of her time," she says. "She foresaw knowledge of computers being essential to seniors. She knew that social isolation was the killer. She knew that creativity was a key thing, along with good nutrition and exercise. These things seem obvious now, but they weren't so much then."

The Center now offers meals in its circular main room (often with someone playing the grand piano), as well as a range of classes. Many tend to encourage creativity (ceramics, music, acting, writing, chair ballet) and are often led by working professionals. Others focus on fitness and are held in the center's little gym and outside it. In-house lectures on philosophy, history, and current affairs are legion.

In her tenure, Horst worked with the senior center's relatively new operator, the nonprofit Sequoia Living, to help continue the center's legacy. Now a volunteer and participant in its ceramics program, Horst remembers a woman wandering in after her husband's death. "She'd spent years caring for him, and was a bit of deer in the headlights. She took this one exercise class, and, with staff encouragement, ultimately became a fitness freak, able to do anything that a 40-year-old could do. This is not uncommon."

The woman also managed to track down a child she'd given up for adoption in her teens, the reunion such a success that she moved to be near this newfound family.

But it's not always so upbeat here. "You're also seeing people through their deaths a lot of the time. Some of them, particularly in the Tenderloin, are coping with severe isolation, poverty, drug use, homelessness." Even so, Horst says the work has ample rewards. She remembers a man coming in, saying he had no friends. He joined an art class and missed a few sessions because of illness. "When he came back, people asked where he'd been. He was so pleased. 'They cared about me, they wanted to know where I was,' he said."

A few blocks away is the Marina Safeway (15 Marina Blvd.). Designed by the architectural firm Wurster, Bernhardt & Emmons and built in 1959, it was the first of many of these groceries to have a curved roofline and a wall of glass fronting the store. (Stores dotted around the continent are called Marina Safeways for their mimicry of this branch.) The store long enjoyed a reputation as one of the city's best pick-up spots, earning the nickname Dateway. For a time, it offered single shoppers a half of the same broken plastic heart, encouraging them to find the shopper who might complete them. Author Armistead Maupin couldn't resist including a fictional version of this event in his Tales of the City, *the first of a series of books that give a great sense of San Francisco from the 1980s on.*

1851

OLDEST SCHOOL

SPRING VALLEY SCIENCE ELEMENTARY SCHOOL

1451 Jackson St.

The oldest school still operating in California, Spring Valley Science Elementary was built in 1851 by a military man from New Hampshire, Col. Thomas Jefferson Nevins, at what is now the corner of Union and Franklin. It was a one-room building, 30 by 20 feet, with a little belfry, and it doubled as a church on Sundays. It sat near a grove of evergreens on the main road between the city's downtown and the Presidio.

In 1852 San Francisco authorized the creation of five public schools to serve its rapidly growing population, purchasing the school from the colonel. It drew 67 pupils in its first year under San Francisco's control. Of those five schools, Spring Valley is the last one remaining.

Back then, the upscale neighborhood now known as Cow Hollow had actual bovines grazing in it. Local historian Hudson Bell quotes from a newspaper of the day: "The air is whitened with bleaching linen . . . the road is lined with milk ranches and henneries, cattle are seen browsing on the scanty herbage of the hills." School picnics were held on a little knoll next to the school, from which one got a view of a cove called Washerwoman's Bay—and it was, in fact, used for laundry.

Coeducational from early on, the school soon outgrew its first house, with a new one built in 1857 on the same lot. In 1861 its then principal J.C. Morrill went off to fight in the Civil War, on the Union side, with his teachers presenting him with a sword, sash, and uniform as a parting gift.

The school grew some more, to 500 children, and moved again in 1868 to a building near Larkin and Polk. In 1884 Chinese immigrants Joseph and Mary Tape, relatively prosperous residents of Cow Hollow, attempted to register their American-born daughter Mamie in the all-White school but were turned away. The couple successfully sued the school board and won, in what would become a landmark antidiscrimination case. But when Mamie went back to register there, she was told she lacked a vaccination certificate and steered towards an exclusively Chinese school.

In recent years there has been renewed interest in the Tape case. One legal historian calls it "one of the most important civil rights decisions that you've probably never heard of." Certainly it was precocious, coming some 70 years before *Brown v. Board of Education*, the Supreme Court's midcentury decision desegregating America's schools.

Lonnie Chin, Spring Valley's principal for three decades, would use the case to talk to the school's children about the importance of fighting for fair treatment. "We want the children to question authority," she told SFGATE, "respectfully."

Most of the students now are from low-income families, about 80 percent of them with English as a second language. Its new principal, Jessica Arnott, says the school is what is known as a World Language school, supplementing its general classes with ones in Spanish and Cantonese. "If the students continue on that path, they can get a certificate of bilingualism."

Staff turnover has been low at Spring Valley for years: "One, two, three, four—I'm the fifth principal in 40 years," Arnott says, counting the names from a board in her office. "We have some longstanding teachers. Considering its place in the city, it's not as well known as you might think. It's more of a hidden gem. Unless people ride by it on the trolley, they often haven't heard of it." With some fanfare and a proclamation from the city, the school recently celebrated its 170th anniversary.

1851

OLDEST BOOKSTORE

BOOKS INC.

Marina: 2251 Chestnut St.

Opera Plaza: 601 Van Ness Ave.

Laurel Village: 3815 California St.

Compass Books: San Francisco Airport, Terminals 2 and 3

This small bookstore chain has roots in the Gold Rush, in a book peddler's sack. Anton Roman was a Bavarian immigrant who struck gold near Shasta City and used the proceeds to begin picking up books in San Francisco to sell to miners in their mountain camps.

Roman soon settled full-time in San Francisco, opening a shop in one of the young city's main business centers, the Montgomery Block. An early ad boasted that it had "for sale the largest and best selected stock of books, in every department of literature, to be found upon the Pacific Coast." In the 1860s he began to publish accounts of Gold Rush–era society in a journal called the *Overland Monthly*, with a logo of a California grizzly standing on the then-new transcontinental railway. It made stars of the newspaperman Mark Twain and of its editor and contributor Bret Harte—Harte's famous short story "The Luck of the Roaring Camp" (published here first) is reportedly derived in part from anecdotes Roman told him.

Not very much is known of its next few owners, but in the 1920s Leon Gelber, a former bookseller for the grand (now gone) department store Emporium, bought the shop with an assist from

Ted Lilienthal, a banker's son. The partners had a small store on Sutter Street, adding an annex at the back with a fireplace that soon became the city's coziest author reading venue.

Longtime owner Lew Lengfeld. Courtesy Books Inc.

Just before the mid-century, the proprietors of Books Inc., then lodged in the Fairmont Hotel, took over. Both Barbara Thompson and Lew Lengfeld were descendants of '49ers, and cultured, competitive Lengfeld was a figure right out of a novel. In the 1950s he hosted the first book-review program on television, and the store began snapping up regional chains throughout the West. A later owner, Michael Tucker, overlapped with Lengfeld toward the end of the older man's years at the helm. "He was the biggest thing on the West Coast," Tucker says. "He was the longtime president of the booksellers' association, until they told him there was a term limit. And then he left the organization."

After Lengfeld's death in the mid-1990s, Tucker and another Michael, Michael Grant, took over the firm. But after the arrival of the big chains Borders and Barnes & Noble, they felt they had no option but to take Books Inc. into bankruptcy in 1997, coming out of it with a leaner operation based entirely in the Bay Area.

Another blow came at the turn of the millennium, when Grant died suddenly of a heart attack. That meant that Tucker had to take on the administrative tasks that Grant had mainly handled. "I got used to it, but I never loved it. What I did love, always, was the people in this field, the relationships you built—that's been the beauty of being in this trade, what was for me this accidental profession."

A few years ago, longtime staffer Andy Perham was appointed his successor as CEO—just as COVID was about to drop. When the store was in lockdown, Perham and his team worked on making the Books Inc. website easier to use, and the store sold nine times more books online in the first year of the outbreak than it had the year before. "That'll remain, we hope, a decent part of our business. But there's still no substitute for being in the store."

Although the micro-chain no longer has that hearth-centered room, the branch near City Hall has a decent-sized back area where major authors come to read. "Author signings don't drive tons of business," Tucker says. "But you do these events, well, because you can, to be part of this great thing."

1979

OLDEST VEGETARIAN RESTAURANT

GREENS

Building A, 2 Marina Blvd.

First-time visitors tend to be impressed, wowed really, with their first sight on entering the restaurant, a sculpture made from the massive bulbous burl that once hung off a redwood tree. It occupies the center of a long, narrow room, with one side all windows. And through those windows they catch sight of the Golden Gate Bridge. For some visitors that's all they notice, that and the food. But some sense something more happening. The servers address you informally, but with elaborate respect. Most have the bodies of regular yoga practitioners, the serenity-now feel and distant look of those who meditate daily.

When my boat-builder father-in-law visited, we brought him here. A cabinet maker by training, he noticed there were no nails in any of the furniture—all the pieces were made using traditional Japanese joinery. (He also had the mid-meal spectacle of a yacht running aground out the window and had to be restrained from heading outside to help.)

This mode of carpentry speaks to what Zen practitioners call The Way, and before she came to Greens, former executive chef Annie Somerville worked at the Tassajara Zen Mountain Center, a retreat founded in 1967, popular with the hippies. For a time Buddhist monks waited tables here, the last one only recently retiring, and the day's tasks have often been doled out to staffers near an altar. This is the Zen strand of the Greens's experience.

And of course, there's a food strand: Greens has had a long relationship with the organic Green Gulch Farm across the Golden Gate Bridge in Marin County. Says the restaurant's current executive chef, Katie Reicher, "Green Gulch is, as its name indicates, in a deep valley, which extends down to the sea. It produces what must be some of the best baby lettuces in the country. And the broccoli and beets . . . " Greens was an early part of the farm-to-table movement, long before it had that name and before everyone was doing it.

Reicher is the latest of four executive chefs in as many decades, all of them women. When Greens was started it was much rarer for a woman to head a kitchen of this size and ambition.

A former nutrition student at Cornell and a graduate of the Culinary Institute of America, Reicher remembers arriving here for the first time before joining the staff in 2015. "I liked how Annie would come down and greet all of the people working here by name, asking about how their kid had done on a test. It just felt so good. I moved from the East to start here on the day I graduated."

In its long tenure as one of America's premier vegetarian restaurants, Greens is credited with mainstreaming fingerling potatoes, golden beets, and arugula. I mention that to Reicher, and she comments, "You know, we aren't obsessed with using trendy ingredients. You won't have the food of the moment, say, the

Impossible Burger, on our menu. First of all, the foods imitating meat—not for us. But also, we're trying for something . . . almost timeless here."

A good restaurant has that ability to take you out of time a bit. My father-in-law has since passed away, but I'll always remember him in this space, his craftsman's eyes figuring out the way the furniture was made. He was shocked at the foolishness of the sailors who'd run their boat aground outside the window, shaking his head in both dismay and delight, a practical person amazed, yet again, at the folly of impractical ones.

Next to Greens there's a picturesque park, Marina Green, and, as you near its Western end this curious apparition comes into view. The Palace of Fine Arts (3601 Lyon St.) was built for the 1915 Pan-Pacific International Exposition by lionized local architect Bernard Maybeck (1862–1957). Here he's riffing on Rome's ancient Temple to Minerva, with a dome on eight piers and long colonnades flanking it. It's a stage set really, originally made of plaster on wood, and it was meant to decay with speed.

*But visitors to the fair loved it, and so it stayed up while the palaces and pavilions around it came down. So beloved was it, that it was nearly entirely reconstructed in the 1960s. Over the years, it's appeared in a great film (*Vertigo*) and a not-so-great one (*So I Married an Axe Murderer*). Its aesthetic has inspired a city on a far-off planet in the* Star Wars *series, and it was the setting for a scene in* Game of Thrones.

1853

OLDEST PRISON COMPLEX

ALCATRAZ

Started as a fort to protect the San Francisco Bay, Alcatraz morphed in the course of the 19th century into a military prison and then into its most famous form, a federal penitentiary. The island's name is an anglicization of the Spanish one, La Isla de Los Alcatraces, the island of the pelicans.

In its three decades as a federal penitentiary, the island was a self-contained little city of the damned. It had its own power plant, factory, market, garden, laundry, library, machine and furniture shops, barbers, baseball field, and tennis court. It was prepared for a long lockdown—and often, when an escape was in progress or when a riot took place, this happened.

There was a spot where well-behaved inmates got to sunbathe; there were tables where they played bridge and dominoes. But there were also tiny cells where prisoners were kept solitary, seeing almost no one for years at a time. Some of America's most famous criminals were confined here. Scarface himself, Al Capone, was a prisoner here—he was, of course, the mob boss whose hired guns took down seven members of a rival Irish gang on St. Valentine's Day in Chicago. Machine Gun Kelly, real name George Kelly Barnes, former Public Enemy Number 1, was confined here for a spree of crimes that included kidnapping a wealthy businessman. A prisoner given the ominous number of 666, the armed robber Willie Radkay, wrote a book (with an extraordinary title) about his time here, *Devil Incarnate: From Altar Boy to Alcatraz.*

Another inmate author was Robert Franklin Stroud, aka the Birdman of Alcatraz. Stroud actually kept his canaries at another prison—Kansas's Leavenworth—and wrote scholarly treatises on the treatment of their diseases. But the screenwriters of the film given Stroud's nickname took dramatic license and brought the birds here, to the Rock.

It was near impossible to escape from the island prison, though 14 attempts were made. The most famous involved some long-term planning. For seven months, inmates Frank Lee Morris and the Anglin Brothers, John and Clarence, scraped around the air-vent in their cells until they could clamber into the ventilation shaft. The absence of the three men wasn't noticed at once because they'd put hand-made dummies in their beds with hair purloined from the barbershop pasted on their mock heads. Though they probably perished in the long swim to shore, it's possible, if highly unlikely, they got away.

The cost of keeping prisoners at Alcatraz was always high—$10 per prisoner per day as compared to $3 elsewhere. (Among other things, water and food had to be shipped over.) It had also become a symbol of something foul—the underside of the American Dream, maybe—by the time then Attorney-General Robert Kennedy closed it in 1963.

It came back into the spotlight in 1969 when a group calling themselves the Indians of All Tribes occupied it to bring attention to the struggles of Native Americans. (Some graffiti remains from that occupation: "Indians Welcome.") A fire during that period also damaged the lighthouse, sometimes called the oldest in the West.

John Martini, author of *Fortress Alcatraz: Guardian of the Golden Gate*, dismisses that claim: "It is near the site of the oldest, built in 1854. That was a relatively short Cape-Cod style lighthouse, and came down when the big prison building went up, because it wasn't tall enough."

The prison is still a foreboding structure. There's still evidence of the famous escape via the air ducts. From one area of the cell-house there's a window facing the city, showing off San Francisco's bright lights at night. That window must have given inmates a tantalizing sense of all the freedoms to be had out there—off the Rock.

Visitors to the city with curious kids often combine a visit to Alcatraz with a stop at The Exploratorium (Pier 15, The Embarcadero). It was founded in 1969 by physicist Frank Oppenheimer, who worked with his brother Robert to build the atomic bomb. After the war, he was drummed out of a professorship at the University of Minnesota by the House Un-American Affairs Committee.

He then taught high school and created this museum, filling it with experiments that turned his students onto science. Interactive exhibits twig ideas about the nature of light, electricity, and human behavior. The docents—called Explainers—are gloriously geeky high-school students.

A local writer called the place "a mad scientist's penny arcade, a scientific funhouse and an experimental laboratory, all rolled into one." And it's got a good bar and restaurant, both with unimpeded views of the Bay, and adults-only nights, with a deejay and light-show in certain rooms.

1852

OLDEST CHOCOLATE COMPANY

GHIRARDELLI CHOCOLATE COMPANY

900 North Point St., Ste. F301

Domenico Ghirardelli was born in 1817 in Rapallo, a picturesque town on Italy's Ligurian coast, and sent off to Genoa to apprentice at Romanengo's, a candy store still in operation. At age 17, the young man witnessed the riots instigated by those wanting to transform Italy into a democracy. Like many at the time, he decided to leave the unrest behind and sailed for South America. There he used what he'd learned to set up his own confectionary stores, first in Uruguay and then in Peru, adopting the Spanish equivalent of his first name, Domingo.

Courtesy Ghirardelli

The owner of a neighboring shop in Lima was a restless Pennsylvania yankee named James Lick, a piano- and cabinet-maker who decided to set sail for California just before gold was found. Lick took along with him some 600 pounds of his friend's chocolate, which he promptly sold, and urged Ghirardelli to join him. (Lick later became one of the state's richest men, endowing an observatory and several local schools.)

One-time president Lyle Ghirardelli works with oversight from his grandfather Domingo's bust. Courtesy Sidney Lawrence

Ghirardelli—pronounced with a hard "G"—had a bumpy start here, losing one of his early stores to fire. Soon enough, though, he had a bustling business on San Francisco's main square, Portsmouth, and became a member of the Vigilance Committee that famously drove a gang of violent criminals out of town.

The business grew steadily over the decades. But it was a minor error in the late 1860s that helped it become an international player. Employees reportedly left semi-processed chocolate hanging in a burlap sack for longer than was normal, and the fatty cocoa butter drained out, leaving behind a dry, powdery residue. These granules dissolved in hot liquids and could be used in baking—and they kept for long periods of time. Ghirardelli began to use what is called the Broma method to make chocolate that could stay fresh when shipped over long distances.

The patriarch died in 1894 on a trip with his daughter back to his seaside hometown in Italy, leaving the company in the hands of his son, also named Domingo. "He was a genius at marketing, plastering the city with billboards," says Sidney Lawrence, great-great grandson of the founder. "He did movie tie-ins, cookbooks for the ladies." It was during his lifetime, in 1923, that the landmark Ghirardelli sign got placed atop the complex—a sign that would be flashed at outgoing navy ships to wish servicemen godspeed.

Courtesy Sidney Lawrence

In the 1960s the company was sold to the food company that produced another San Francisco treat, Rice-a-Roni. Meanwhile, a shipping heir named William Matson Roth, oversaw a sensitive conversion of the factory complex to an indoor-outdoor urban mall—and it is here, still, that Ghirardelli's flagship shop and soda fountain serves up sundaes named for Twin Peaks and Emperor Norton, a longtime local character.

In the late 1990s the Swiss chocolate company Lindt & Sprüngli became the owner. On its watch, Ghirardelli introduced the squares that would become its signature, with fillings as diverse as blueberries and bourbon. It also became one of the first chocolate companies to advertise the percentages of cacao in each bar on the package, a now-widespread practice. Recently opened is the Ghirardelli Chocolate Experience (900 North Point St.), which offers hands-on lessons in the science and craft of chocolate making.

The last of those bearing the Ghirardelli name died in 1991. Gone but not forgotten. On loan to the National Portrait Gallery, the founder's bust sits in a room with representations of such famous Americans as Henry James, Mary Cassatt, and Mark Twain.

WEST OF VAN NESS

PACIFIC HEIGHTS, THE RICHMOND, THE FILLMORE,
THE WESTERN ADDITION, THE PRESIDIO

1852

OLDEST PRIVATE HIGH SCHOOL

SACRED HEART CATHEDRAL PREPARATORY

1055 Ellis St.

The name is an amalgam of the two Catholic high schools that joined in 1987: Sacred Heart, a boys' school, and Cathedral, for girls. Together they formed the first co-ed Catholic high school in San Francisco. Both have roots back in the 19th century, making this the oldest private high school in the city.

The girls' school was founded first, in 1852, and was initially named St. Vincent's for one of the founders of the order of nuns that ran the school. An order started in the 17th century in Paris by St. Vincent de Paul and St. Louise De Marillac, the Daughters of Charity came to San Francisco at the invitation of then-Archbishop Joseph Alemany, who saw a need for teachers in a booming city. Of the seven nuns who set out from Maryland, two died of cholera en route. The others, with their winged, white wimples, got down to work.

The boys' school, Sacred Heart, was founded in 1868 and run by the Christian Brothers, another 18th-century order, this one founded by St. John Baptist de la Salle.

A rivalry between Sacred Heart's team, long known as the Fightin' Irish, and the players from another boy's Catholic School, St. Ignatius, began with a rugby game played on St. Patrick's Day, 1893. The Irish eked out a victory. Since then, the St. Ignatius teams have won the majority of the interschool games. In what is claimed to be the oldest high-school athletic rivalry west of the Mississippi, the two schools' boys' teams still compete each year in football, baseball, and basketball.

Mark Pardini is the school's director of communications and marketing and an alum. He was student body president just after the school went co-ed. "Like most births, there can be a lot of pain, but . . . look what happened." The school draws students from all over the Bay Area, with about 1,100 applying for 300 spots in each year's ninth-grade class. The tuition in a recent year was $22,000—about $7,000 less than at fancier St. Ignatius.

Courtesy Sacred Heart Cathedral Preparatory

Most students at Sacred Heart receive some form of financial aid, and about half the students are non-White. On many weekdays, a cadre of students in their khakis and polo shirts can be seen crossing Van Ness to go volunteer at St. Anthony's, the longtime soup kitchen and aid organization in the Tenderloin.

Most of Sacred Heart's students go on to postsecondary education, some at the nation's elite institutions. "But also, we have a lot of students who are the first in their family to go to college, the first generation to speak English," Pardini says. "For some of them, a place like Sonoma State will serve them better than Stanford." The school has traditionally sent a lot of graduates to St. Mary's across the Bay.

The school has a few famous alums, including baseball Hall of Famer Joe Cronin, Olympian Shannon Rowbury, and former San

Francisco mayor Joe Alioto. Alumni loyalty helped build a new $16-million student-life center with a big new gym and dining hall. But Sacred Heart Cathedral Prep occupies a tight space, and the school has to send its football team elsewhere to train. This is one of the reasons it was a big surprise when the football team took home, for the first time, the state championship in 2022. "It's a meat-grinder, their division," says Pardini, "the toughest athletic league in Northern California. With them commuting to the practice field—it's all the more remarkable what this team did."

A few blocks away from Sacred Heart is a successor to the oldest nursery school and kindergarten in the West, the Phoebe Hearst Preschool (1315 Ellis St.). Its predecessor was founded by legendary educator Sarah B. Cooper, a follower of Friedrich Froebel, who helped start the international kindergarten movement, opening the first one in Germany in 1840s.

Cooper started her school in 1879, taking 12 children off the streets of the Barbary Coast and teaching them for free. She also convinced two of the region's wealthiest women, Phoebe Hearst and Jane Stanford, to back her Golden Gate Kindergarten Association. For a time, both women had separate preschools named for them, but when they were merged, Hearst's name won out. An arts-oriented preschool, it was run at the mid-century by Rhoda Kellogg, who wrote popular books about the uses of art in early childhood development and collected about 500,000 pieces of art created by children around the world.

1886

OLDEST VICTORIAN HOUSE OPEN TO THE PUBLIC

HAAS-LILIENTHAL HOUSE

2007 Franklin St.

The Haas-Lilienthal house is a Queen Anne–style fantasia, with a turret with what is known as a witch's hat on top. From a balcony up high, the family that lived here once watched the city burn after the 1906 quake and worried that the fire would come for them. It stopped a mere block away.

There are older houses in San Francisco, but none that speak so eloquently of the city's post–Gold Rush heyday. And it's the oldest house that's open to the public. Constructed in 1886 by grocery wholesaler William Haas, its 11,500 square feet are divided into 24 rooms. When Haas's daughter Alice died in 1972, the family gave the pile to San Francisco Heritage, a nonprofit devoted to historic preservation. Most of the furnishings came with it, as well as an organ, a player piano, and a Victrola. It has the sailor suits and sundresses worn by the kids who grew up here and the dollhouses and miniature trains they played with.

As you enter, you pass the grandfather clock chiming out the half hours. You then proceed from the mahogany-paneled front parlor through pocket doors to the second parlor, and then through another set of doors to a dining room kitted out in golden oak. In that room the attentive will also spot the only indication that the family who lived here was Jewish: a Sabbath Lamp.

Haas was born in a small town in Bavaria called Reckendorf, the youngest of 10 children who, according to antisemitic German law, could not legally marry. Arriving in San Francisco in the 1860s, he joined a cousin's grocery business, worked hard, and did well. As it turned out, Haas was one of several Jewish immigrants from that small Bavarian town to make good here, with financier Isaias Hellman among the others. Together the group was known locally as the Reckendorfers.

Past the dining room is his office, his ad hoc business headquarters when his firm's downtown offices burned down after the quake. Next to that are the butler's pantry and the kitchen, with its 1920s-era, eight-burner range. On the kitchen wall there's a device right out of *Downton Abbey*, an enunciator, which has little switches next to a list of the house's rooms; when family pushed a button in those rooms, servants would know they were wanted there. A plaque reads: "In loving memory of Cook Tillie Richter, Nursemaid Frieda Wiedmann, Waitress Annemarie Schulz, Chauffeur Morton Vrang, and all others who devotedly served this house and family over nine decades."

On the second story are the family bedrooms, comfy rather than grand, though one has a Tiffany lamp in it. There's also a bathroom equipped with a bidet. On the story above that are the Spartan maid's quarters, a sink in each, since all the staff shared a single bathroom. Also up there but closed to visitors now is the balcony from which they all watched the fire approach.

A smaller house across the drive was built to house two Haas children

orphaned when William's son Charles and his wife Fannie died young. The two kids, Billy and Madeleine, lived there with their nurse and driver. The main house ultimately came to be occupied by Haas's daughter Alice and her husband Samuel Lilienthal, who would become a partner in the grocery firm.

A condition the family attached to the gift of the house was that they be allowed to reassemble here every Christmas eve to celebrate. For the rest of us, one time to go is at Halloween, when it turns itself into a spooky mansion, haunted by the ghosts of its rich past.

The oldest house in the city, the Treat House (1266 Hampshire St.) was built by Gold Rush pioneers George and John Treat in 1849. It's a simple two-story, and the years have not been kind to it. Nonetheless, in San Francisco's overheated real-estate market, it recently sold with an asking price of $1.5 million.

The Abner Phelps House (1111 Oak St.) was built between 1850 and 1852. Phelps worked as a lawyer in San Francisco, commuting to his office by horse. It's often said that he built it in New Orleans and shipped it here to please his Southern wife, but there's no evidence to back that claim.

Neither home is open to the public; both speak of a utilitarian era, when you built to have some shelter over your head in a boomtown that was going up fast.

1849

OLDEST JEWISH FAITH COMMUNITIES

CONGREGATION SHERITH ISRAEL

2266 California St.

TEMPLE EMANU-EL

2 Lake St.

Congregation Sherith Israel

This synagogue was founded by an Eastern European contingent, particularly immigrants from the territories that would become Poland. It has twice moved westward from downtown as the city expanded in the same direction. Though born Orthodox, it shifted towards Reform under charismatic rabbi Jacob Lieto, with men and women worshipping together and the wearing of the kippah optional.

The congregation's home since 1905 is among the city's most spectacular buildings, with a huge dome topping a sanctuary with 20,000 cubic feet of space. Instead of facing east towards Jerusalem, as was traditional, it faces north to catch the most light, which it supplements with 1,100 electric bulbs.

The building's Mexican-American architect, Albert Pissis, also contributed the Hibernia Bank (in Mid-Market) and the James Flood mansion (atop Nob Hill) to the cityscape, and his brother Emile did some of the synagogue's stained glass. One of his windows depicts what congregants call "Movie-Star Moses" bearing his Ten Commandments. What's behind him is not Sinai, but Yosemite's Half

Dome and El Capitan. The observant can also find what are likely San Francisco's Twin Peaks and Dolores Park. Gordon Gladstone, Sherith Israel's Executive Director, says, "People frequently say the window reflects a view that this, California, is our promised land."

The temple came through the 1906 quake with minor damage. Afterwards it served for a time as the city's courthouse, bearing witness to a show trial of the city's mayor for corruption. The building also emerged from the 1989 quake with only cosmetic damage. Still, the city recently required it and other buildings of its vintage to do seismic retrofits, something Sherith Israel managed, at a cost of $16 million, while also installing LED lightbulbs in the sanctuary. Another recent priority for this congregation with roots in Eastern Europe has been helping Russian Jewish refugees to settle into the city.

The congregation recently hired its first female senior rabbi, Jessica Zimmerman, a Talmudic scholar who has a doctorate in astrophysics. It also brought on board, as cantor, David Frommer, a former soldier with the Israeli forces who later served as the first cantor chaplain in the US army.

"This area of the Fillmore was once predominantly Jewish," Gladstone says. "Then it became Japanese, at least until the mass internment in the War. Then it became predominantly African American, with all the jazz clubs and other businesses here. The building has seen a lot of changes in its time."

Temple Emanu-El

Disagreements over the appropriate ritual helped divide the early community, but so did class differences. The founding members of Emanu-El were often German-American Jews who had been here longer than their Eastern European coreligionists and had a more established financial position. Where Sherith Israel congregants, at one point, paid annual dues of $35, those at Emanu-El contributed $100.

Unlike Sherith Israel, Emanu-El was hit hard by the 1906 quake, its Gothic Revival synagogue gutted in the fire and its library, archives, and historic torah destroyed. Though the congregation repaired its Sutter Street home enough that services could be held for a few years, the building lost its onion-shaped domes. Emanu-El's elders soon hired one of the city's leading architects, Arthur Brown Jr., to build them something new. The designer of City Hall and the Opera House, Brown did a spare, sculptural essay in steel and concrete in the city's Western reaches, completing it in 1926.

Its central space, monumental and domed, is less ornamented than Sherith Israel's. But its details, though fewer, pack a punch—it is fronted, for instance, by fancy brass doors representing the 12 tribes of Israel, sculpted in a streamlined Deco style by artists George Dennison and Frank Ingerson.

Emanu-El is one of the first eight temples in the US to declare itself officially Reform, and its rabbis have often found national prominence. An early rabbi, Elkan Cohn, was one of those who, before emigrating, took to the barricades in his native

Germany in 1848 to push for a new politics. In San Francisco he sought to find a way, in the words of the Psalms, for him and his congregants to sing unto the Lord a new song.

Music has long mattered here. In 1884, Emanu-El became the first American synagogue to hire a female cantor, the internationally known opera singer Julie Rosewald, after her husband, also a cantor, died. A later cantor, Reuben Rinder, composed a corpus of distinguished music while also mentoring two of the 20th century's greatest violinists, Yehudi Menuhin and Isaac Stern.

Both Emanu-El and Sherith Israel have solid charitable traditions. In fact, the communities that founded them set up organizations to aid new arrivals before they built synagogues.

Several people with individual or family connections to Temple Emanu-El have had exhibits at the Contemporary Jewish Museum (736 Mission St.). One focused on the cultural impact of the jeans manufactured by congregant Levi Strauss, while two others looked at people who brought music to the masses: Bill Graham, the man who filled San Francisco's Fillmore with the top acts of the 1960s, and Warren Hellman, who more recently helped found the popular local festival Hardly Strictly Bluegrass, a now-annual event in Golden Gate Park. The museum inhabits an old power station right downtown—a brick building, a rarity for San Francisco, completed in 1881. It has an annex attached to it, a massive glass and steel crystal-like structure designed by Daniel Libeskind, producing, from a certain angle, a visual of the two Hebrew letters that together form the word for life.

1850

OLDEST FUNERAL HOME

MCAVOY, O'HARA & EVERGREEN MORTUARY

4545 Geary Blvd.

The founding date of this funeral home is approximate. It seems likely that the first owners, the French-Canadian Beaudry brothers, started the business in the 1840s, borrowing a stagecoach to serve as a hearse, but 1850 is a generally accepted start date. Certainly, by the time of the Gold Rush, the brothers, led by the magnificently named Louis-Napoléon Beaudry, were in the area and ready to administer funerary rites. The brothers did well, purchasing their own carriage and livery and bringing on board young Hugh McAvoy, the son of Irish emigrant farmers, in the 1870s.

By 1904, McAvoy was ready to retire and hired a young Irishman, Daniel O'Hara, who had connections here. At the mid-century, O'Hara passed the business on to his only son. In charge until the 1990s, Daniel O'Hara Jr. witnessed and helped drive big changes in the industry. The youngest-ever president of the California Funeral Directors' Association, he had the job of responding to the critique by investigative journalist Jessica Mitford in her book, *The American Way of Death*. Published in 1963, the bestseller was critical of the industry's lack of pricing transparency, and the ways in which some funeral homes took advantage of the bereaved. O'Hara helped get regulations on the books setting standards for prearranging funerals and disclosing the price ranges of different caskets.

Late in the 20th century Junior in turn passed the business along to his two sons, Daniel III and Richard. "There are seven of us O'Haras working here now," Daniel O'Hara III says. "My daughter Olga, our wives. If you add up the years all of us have been doing this it comes to more than 300."

Now in her early 40s, Daniel's daughter Olga has been working in the business since she was 16 and laughs at comparisons of her clan to the fictional family that ran a funeral home in the hit TV drama *Six Feet Under*. But she's serious about the work. "Death is chaotic, the people we meet are thrown into disruption. It's a time of uncertainty, fear and loss. You can't prepare for it." Many Yelp reviews mention her expertise at tracking down the paperwork someone needs, say, to take a dead relative's ashes to Taiwan, or to get the Medical Examiner's office to release a corpse. That is certainly a part of the job, but the more important one, she says, is to respond to grieving people's needs. "When a woman who's lost her husband of 30 years wants to speak to you for hours and hours on the phone, it's a privilege. Our job is to turn what can be the most difficult experience of many people's lives into something . . . manageable. Even to help them find some of the love and beauty in it."

Courtesy McAvoy, O'Hara, Evergreen

For his part, Daniel says he's tried to embody certain principles in his work over the last five decades, ones that were passed down to him: "Take care of your grieving families and be honest, be yourself." Even while he's tried to put these ideals into practice, he's developed a keen eye for the business's details. When pop star Michael Jackson died in 2009, longtime *San Francisco Chronicle* columnist Leah Garchik asked Daniel for a comment on the arrangements. He clocked the singer's coffin as an Indiana-made Promethean casket of solid bronze with 14-karat gold-plated hardware, retailing for upwards of $25,000. But one thing shocked him: The coffin did not have a catafalque under it to support it. Though money had clearly been no object, there ought to have been a catafalque.

There are very few dead people buried in San Francisco: The lion's share of them are in a town south of San Francisco, Colma. By one recent estimate, the so-called City of the Dead has just under 1,500 living inhabitants and 1.5 million corpses. Among the latter are lawman Wyatt Earp and newspaper baron William Randolph Hearst.

Long ago, San Francisco's Western reaches had four large cemeteries. But the city grew, and there was increasing pressure to replace the graves with housing. The city banned new burials in 1903, and, one by one, the cemeteries left for Colma, the bodies disinterred and moved.

Left behind is the neoclassical San Francisco Columbarium (1 Lorraine Ct.), built by architect Bernard Cahill in 1897. Under a wide dome the cremated remains of 30,000 people are lodged, often in vases and niches. There's a small memorial to assassinated city supervisor Harvey Milk, but the actual location of his ashes remains a closely guarded secret.

1855

OLDEST UNIVERSITY

UNIVERSITY OF SAN FRANCISCO

2130 Fulton St.

The city's oldest university, founded by Jesuit Priests, offers over 300 graduate and undergraduate programs on its 55-acre campus. Consecrated in 1914, its grand, two-towered church, St. Ignatius, stands on a hilltop, one of the city's great landmarks.

Its current president, Father Paul Fitzgerald, SJ, is a learned man. The recipient of various magna and summa cum laude degrees, he's published on a wide variety of subjects. But he's also plainspoken, practical. "The church was built after the quake and fire destroyed our earlier buildings. It has so much steel in its frame that it's still been assessed as safe, seismically. It's where our students begin their journey and where they end it, with convocation. It's the heart of our campus."

On its opening day, in 1855, the university had, for the last time, a 1:1 student-faculty ratio, with three teachers and three students. The priest who founded it, Father Michael Accolti, SJ, had a dim opinion of the Gold Rush–era city when he arrived here. He later recalled: "Whether it should be called a madhouse or Babylon, I am at a loss to determine; so great in those days was the disorder, the brawling, the open immorality." The fathers had their work cut out for them.

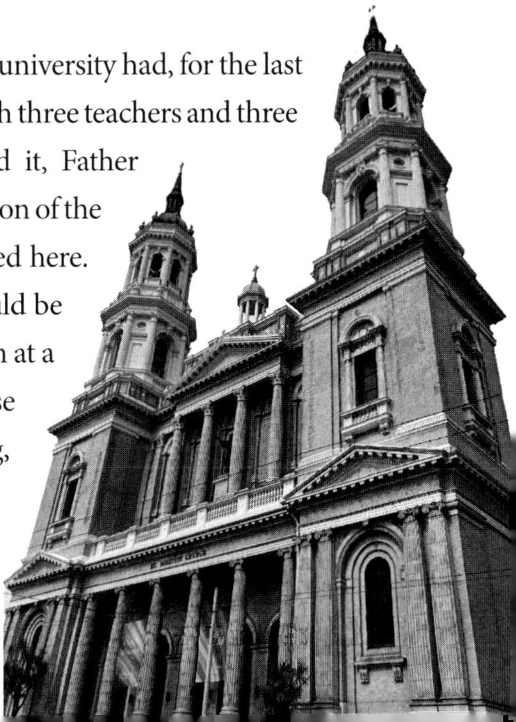

An early ad touted both liberal-arts classes and preprofessional training like bookkeeping and penmanship. And that mix has remained, with training for law, business, and nursing on offer, along with classes in philosophy and history. The college has had four different sites in the city: a smallish one on Market Street in its early years; a large, beautiful one at Hayes and Van Ness (the one destroyed by the quake and fire); a temporary one further west on Hayes (called the Shirt Factory for its plain, industrial look); and, finally, this one, with an adjunct added, the so-called Lone Mountain campus, in 1978.

In the 1930s USF became one of the first schools in the nation to field mixed-race teams. In 1951 it had one of the nation's best football teams, an undefeated, united squad, When it was invited to the Orange Bowl on the condition it field only White players, the team refused to play. Its basketball program produced one of the all-time great pros, the late, lamented Bill Russell. "Sports give this opportunity to overcome racism," Fitzgerald says, "We integrated our teams years before courts ordered it. . . . We want to teach not just intercultural competency here, but humility, awe before people from other backgrounds."

The University now has roughly the same numbers of Black, Latino, Asian, and White students in attendance, and is moderately hard to get into—over 60 percent of an admittedly pretty qualified applicant pool for undergrad make the cut.

This part of the city gets more than its share of fogs off the Pacific, giving the school newspaper its cute name, *The Foghorn*. The paper had the signal distinction of graduating Pierre Salinger in the mid-century, who went on to edit the *Chronicle* and serve as press secretary to President Kennedy. Other recent graduates of note include dearly beloved children's book author Tomie dePaola and San Francisco mayor London Breed, the city's first Black woman mayor.

The school has also placed a high priority on environmental fitness, meeting its goal of becoming carbon neutral some 30 years before the deadline it set itself of 2050. Fitzgerald outlines the steps large and small the school has taken, from using energy-efficient washing machines to making its natural-gas interior heating system also warm the water. "Our dining hall is down to one freezer," says Fitzgerald. "Freezers aren't great for the climate. And it's for ice cream."

Another old institution founded by a Catholic religious order sits across the street from the University of San Francisco's St. Ignatius Parish Church. Founded in 1857, St. Mary's (450 Stanyan St.), is the oldest continuously operating hospital in the city and was first set up by the Sisters of Mercy. The young city's archbishop sent a request to the sisters in Dublin, and eight of the volunteers were selected. But the boat was overbooked, so they sailed out of Liverpool instead. Good thing, because the ship they were booked on collided with another one mid-Atlantic, and everyone perished.

The hospital's current main building is a behemoth built in the 1970s in the International Modernist style, and it has about as much character as an uncooked block of tofu. Never mind; from the start St. Mary's has provided medical care to the poor, and its medics staff the clinic treating sick travelers at the San Francisco Airport.

1918

OLDEST HAT MAKER

PAUL'S HAT WORKS

6128 Geary Blvd.

Paul's Hat Works was founded by a Peruvian immigrant to San Francisco named Napoleon Marquez—people called him Paul for reasons now unknown. He passed the store along to an apprentice, who passed it along to another, and so on, through about six master hatters for over 100 years down to its current proprietor, Abbie Dwelle. The shop's lore, either developed by "Paul" or accrued over time, is that a good hat often takes 24 steps and can be turned around in 30 days.

To measure a head's dimensions, Dwelle puts a contraption called a Conformiture over the client's head. This invention from the mid-19th century has lots of little rods inside a boater-hat shape that mold to match the shape of the head underneath it. Then the best material and look are debated: Would the client go for a bowler? A porkpie? A fedora? The ever-popular fedoras come in versions named for the different parts of the city—the North Beach being well-suited for the bohemian boulevardier, the Financial District one being, well, all biz.

Once the type of hat has been decided, blocks of the correct size and shape are used to shape the crown. Then flat irons, steamers, and flanges are deployed to give the brim the appropriate look. Next up are the all-important dents (on the hats that should have them). The leather sweat bands are added inside, the ribbon out. Then in goes the label, which features a hatted individual against the San Francisco skyline, with the motto "Paul's Hat Works: When it Pours, We Reign."

The tiny shop is crammed with a collection of nostalgia-inducing old hatboxes, as well as a sign advising, "Please handle hats by the brim not the crown." The prices are agreed between hatter and client, but have traditionally ranged from about $300 to $2,000. Former owner Michael Harris had one Panama he said he wouldn't let go for less than $30,000—his 38 years of running the business have earned him a photo on one packed wall.

Harris was prepared to close it all down in 2008, when a group of four young women, Dwelle among them, decided they'd take it on. "We made hats for fun before buying the shop," Dwelle says. "Not at the quality level of Paul's. But we had a lot of costume-making skills." With help, the four of them learned their ways around the old machines. There was much publicity generated by these women coming into what had long been a male preserve. "As we blend masculine and feminine and admit the giant gray area in between," says Dwelle, "there's not a men's hat and a women's hat. I make hats for anyone brave enough to wear them."

By 2014, the foursome had realized it wasn't easy for all of them to live on the takings of a necessarily small business. And Dwelle decided to continue on her own.

The vegan has had to make her peace with using felt made from beaver and rabbit fur. "Wool doesn't keep its shape as well, doesn't remember as much." A few years ago a longstanding client, the novelist and Grammy-nominated jazz producer Robert Mailer Anderson, asked if the store would make a hat for his friend Barack Obama, and a picture of the pair of them, together in Paul's hats, hangs on a wall.

For Dwelle, there's a psychological element to what she does. "When a client puts on a hat that works, it brings out their facial characteristics, their shoulders, their height—and something more. They're striking. You don't mistake them for the other guy on the street."

A couple of storefronts West of Paul's is Trad'r Sam (6150 Geary Blvd.), the world's oldest continually operating Tiki bar. It isn't fancy; the interior is long on rattan, short on phony South Pacific idols. The drinks aren't made with artisanal liqueurs. They're mainly the same as they were from the start—a Hurricane, a Zombie, a Scorpion Bowl to share. Sam's is a congenial neighborhood dive bar with tiki accents.

The seat of fancy Tiki in the city is The Tonga Room & Hurricane Club (950 Mason St.) in the basement of the Fairmont Hotel. Popular with conventioneers and hipsters from the Mission, it has grass huts, lava-rock walls, faux thunderstorms, gigantic idols, and an island in the middle of a swimming pool disguised as a tropical lagoon. Periodically, Tonga's closing will be mooted, until there's an outcry, with long petitions presented to anyone with influence.

1776

OLDEST FORT COMPLEX

PRESIDIO

1750 Lincoln Blvd.

Not much remains of the fort the Spanish planted at the tip of the San Francisco peninsula in 1776. It was, from the start, a bit of a shambles, a stretch too far for an empire in decline. Spain sent ancient cannons up from Peru (still here), but there was no need of them for years—none of the other so-called great colonial powers much wanted this rather sandy headland.

Spain would eventually build a small military installation and call it Castillo de San Joaquin, but didn't pay the few soldiers who manned it for years. The Mexicans who threw off the Spanish yoke in 1821 had even less interest in making a go of this far-flung post, one year paying the few soldiers in cigarettes. An American expedition led by John Fremont basically took the sleepy fort without a shot in 1846.

What we see now is mainly the American fort, today's Parade Lawn, in what is called the Main Post. It has the dimensions of the Spanish fort, and the path Spaniards took between the Presidio and Mission (south of here) is known as Lover's Lane. Next to the longtime officer's club at the head of the Parade Lawn are a few adobe bricks with a plaque that claims, falsely, that they belonged to the oldest building in the city—most historians agree that the Mission is older.

With the discovery of gold in California in 1849 San Francisco became a place worth having, and the diligent Americans turned what had been a fort in name into a fort in fact, filling its roughly three square miles with over 800 buildings. By the Civil War the Americans had replaced what remained of Castillo de San Joaquin with the more formidable Fort Point, a sea fort the Golden Gate Bridge builders preserved by arching the suspension bridge right over it. (It's best known as the place where Kim Novak's character in the Alfred Hitchcock film *Vertigo* throws herself into the surf, causing Jimmy Stewart to leap to the rescue.)

The basic brick barracks lived in by the rank-and-file line were at the western end of the parade grounds. The officers' houses—elegant Victorians—are some distance, style-wise and physically, from the quarters of the men. Rob Thompson, a federal Preservation Officer who works at the Presidio, comments: "You can read the entrenched hierarchy of the army in the architecture."

The oldest preserved block of Victorians in the city, most dating from the 1860s, lines Funston Avenue, named for one of the Presidio's most legendary generals, "Fighting" Fred Funston, who earned the nickname in the Spanish-American and Philippine-American wars. His equally esteemed successor, General John Pershing, also lived here in a big house opposite the officers' club. That house burned down in a fire that took the lives of Pershing's wife and two of his children in 1915 when the general was in Mexico pursuing insurgent Pancho Villa. Pershing went on to serve in the World War I along with many who enlisted and were trained at the Presidio. Its hospital treated over 12,000 of those who got wounded or sick in Europe.

Some of those who didn't make it through or who died in combat are among the 30,000 buried in the San Francisco National Cemetery, their white headstones arranged in parallel lines. Long cut off from the Parade Lawn by an elevated highway built to access the Golden Gate Bridge, the graveyard is now walkable via the new Presidio Tunnel Tops park. From the park you can also reach a re-wilded part of Crissy Field, the former airfield at the Presidio—it's becoming the swamp it was long ago. It all seems a version of the bible verse about turning swords into plowshares in peacetime, making parade grounds into parks, military airfields into wetlands.

The Presidio has had baseball diamonds, polo grounds, football fields, boxing gyms, and what Federal Preservation officer Rob Thompson says is probably the city's oldest tennis court not far from the Parade Lawn.

It has what is certainly San Francisco's oldest golf club, The Presidio Golf Course and Clubhouse (300 Findley Rd.), founded in 1895. San Francisco native Joe DiMaggio was a member. "He was good off the tee," a friend said, "but his short game [was] inconsistent. Now I know why he never bunted."

It also has Presidio Bowl and Grill (93 Moraga Ave.), the city's oldest alley. It's a successor to a business founded perhaps, as long ago as 1911. Its owner, former competitive bowler Victor Meyerhoff, remembers bidding on the bowling concession at age 22. "I hadn't had many big jobs by that point. I remember getting my proposal all photocopied up at Kinko's, thinking they'd never have me. But here I am."

1919

OLDEST LETTERPRESS PRINTER

ARION PRESS

1802 Hays St.

The Arion Press and the printing business from which it grew, The Grabhorn Press, have produced just under 800 books in over a century—a small output, but many of them are works of astounding beauty. In 19th-century San Francisco, printing came second only to shipping as an industry. This press preserves some of the old technologies and techniques used in that period.

The process takes place, from start to finish, under one roof, in an old steam-generation plant on the edge of the Presidio. It begins with molten metal, lead mainly, bubbling in a vat. The lead is then molded into "sorts" in the shapes of various letters and characters. ("The expression 'out of sorts' may come from that," says Arion's creative director and lead printer Blake Riley.) Staff then arrange these "sorts" into "pages," which are then put into "chases"—steel frames—and these are tightened—"locked down" and applied to paper.

Arion's recently retired head, Andrew Hoyem, learned such terms in the 1960s and '70s from one of the Grabhorn brothers, Robert—whose machinery Arion took over. The overarching approach he took from his mentor was something called "allusive printing." According to this philosophy, all of the aesthetic choices that go into making a book, including the illustrations and fonts chosen, should be inspired by the text.

Courtesy Erik Carlson

The most famous book done by the Grabhorns was their version of Walt Whitman's *Leaves of Grass*. Printed in 1930, it's an oversized book with an unfussy type. Illustrated with woodcuts, it's got a red, goatskin spine and a mahogany cover. "The most perfect book we ever printed," was brother Edwin Grabhorn's not-so-humble brag.

Their disciple, Hoyem was born in South Dakota and grew up all over the West. As a boy he liked both to draw and write. Soon after arriving in San Francisco, he began to work with the Auerhahn Press, a publisher of many of the so-called Beat writers who put San Francisco on the literary map. Since joining Arion he's also printed many sumptuous versions of American classics. Collectors lavish praise on Arion's 1979 edition of *Moby Dick*—it is printed on blue-grey paper of a vaguely marine aspect with a whale watermarked into it. Arion also did a bible in 1998—one copy of which has gone to Grace Cathedral up on Nob Hill. "It's probably the last bible that will be produced using hot-metal typesetting," says Ted Gioia, Arion's program and development director.

Hoyem often had the press pair artists with writers. And so Robert Motherwell illustrated an Arion edition of James Joyce's magnum opus *Ulysses*. Published in 1988, one recently sold at Christie's for $5,625. More recently, Audrey Niffeneger collaborated with Margaret Atwood on a book of satiric verse, *The Morte de Smudgie*, and leading Latin-American artists contributed to a volume of Pablo Neruda sonnets. This is a revival of the 19th-century tradition of producing books that marry art and writing—*livre d'artiste* was the French term for these volumes. The New York Museum of Modern

Art featured three Arion editions in an exhibit of the 100 most beautiful books published in the last century.

In this tech-mad city, does Arion have a future? Riley once commented, "The Internet has relieved the burden of the encyclopedia from the book, liberating it to be its sparkly self." This formulation leaves the task of conveying masses of information speedily to the Internet, but still sees a special future for the book. The late Anthony Bourdain once did a feature on Arion for a show on those who master time-honored crafts. In it, he sniffs an Arion book approvingly, and then lifts it up and down: "There's a heft to this. You know this is a well-made thing."

Across town in Potrero Heights, the San Francisco Center for the Book (375 Rhode Island St.) also deploys old printing technology, but uses it to teach the basics of bookbinding and letter-press printing. Founded in 1996, it is the oldest such center on the West Coast, with classes that book up months in advance. Here are big paper guillotines and terrifying shears, hammers to help in the binding process, stoves for heating glue, and several presses from the pre-offset era.

The classes are hands-on. Students in binding classes move from making pamphlets to travel notebooks to book-books. Those who take the printing class go from making monochrome cards, to small duotone broadsides, to big multi-colored posters. One rarefied class even teaches students how to make the wax tablets used by the classical Romans. Students who demonstrate a level of mastery of the machines and craft can book time to work independently here.

1863

OLDEST SEASIDE PLEASURE GROUNDS

CLIFF HOUSE & SUTRO BATHS

1090 Point Lobos Ave.

Twenty-five years a park ranger for the Golden Gate National Recreation Area, John Martini occasionally guides a tour of the oldest seaside pleasure grounds in the city, drawing heavily on the histories he's written of this area. This cliff-lined promontory just north of Ocean Beach is known both as Land's End and Point Lobos. This is the site of the old Sutro Baths, once the largest indoor swimming complex in the world and now a popular space for a wander, as evidenced by the often-full parking lot next to it. "San Francisco's favorite ruins," Martini says, pointing at a bride and groom being photographed on a seawall, a yoga class downward-dogging on a flat surrounded by wild fennel.

The tour's starting point is Cliff House, the latest restaurant of that name to stand on this site. "It's the most incendiary landmark in San Francisco," he says, "having burned down twice, blew up once. It was closed during WWI, Prohibition, the Depression, in COVID. But it always keeps bouncing back."

The first Cliff House, though a simple roadhouse, was one with a view that drew three US presidents and well-to-do people like the Hearsts, Stanfords, and Crockers. Enter brash, ambitious Adolph Sutro. A Jewish immigrant from Germany who came here in the mid-19th century, he got rich by helping get the silver in

Nevada's legendary Comstock Lode out of the ground. Returning to San Francisco with a pile, he began buying up much of the city's as-yet undeveloped Western reaches. He also bought Cliff House, by then a seedy shadow of its former self. In 1887, a schooner carrying dynamite foundered near it, exploding and taking out the building's north half, with the remainder burning up on Christmas Eve in 1894.

Sutro, meanwhile, had developed a grandiose plan to redevelop the whole oceanfront. Inspired, he said, by a tidal pool, he started work on an aquarium that would bring creatures and water in from the Pacific. From there grew the idea of a vast set of baths. "A small

Public domain

place would not satisfy me," he told a reporter. "I must have it, large and pretentious, in keeping with the heights and the great ocean itself." In the end the tanks would hold nearly 2 million gallons, with 25,000 people gamboling in the complex.

In the mid-1890s Sutro also had builders putting up a fancier Cliff House, an eight-story house of many turrets. The floors above the pools he filled with a strange miscellany of objects: mummies and sarcophagi, a stuffed polar bear, a taxidermy version of the massive sea lion who used to lord it over Seal Rock. He opened the whole complex to great fanfare in 1896. It was at once a hit—except with a man named John Harris, who was told he could not swim here because he was Black. He successfully sued, one of the first such victories in the country.

A mere two years after its opening, an addled Sutro died, leaving his daughter to manage it all. On her watch, Cliff House would burn down again in 1907, and she'd order a straightforward neoclassical building erected in 1909 that is still standing today. The baths would go up in flames in 1966. The ruins gained in grooviness when they appeared in the 1971 counterculture classic, *Harold and Maude*, and the National Parks Service purchased the remnants of Sutro's swim palace (along with Cliff House) in the late 1970s.

THE HAIGHT-ASHBURY

1967

OLDEST FREE CLINIC

HAIGHT ASHBURY FREE CLINICS

558 Clayton St.

The long and winding road that led to the nation's first free medical clinic started in Oklahoma. Dave Smith's family were Okies who fled the Dust Bowl in the Depression. Many were stopped at the border of California and told they weren't wanted. Even so, the Smiths made their way to Bakersfield, the gateway to the Central Valley. Orphaned at 19, Dave studied at Berkeley, went to medical school at the University of San Francisco, landed an internship at San Francisco General, and joined the exclusive Olympic Club. He was on his way.

"But something happened," he says. For one thing, he was interested in experimental pharmaceuticals as a scientist and even tried LSD. Most of the city's hospitals took a hard line on addiction, sending those who were on bad trips away. A municipal official wanted to put a banner on the Bay Bridge reading "Hippies Not Welcome."

Word got out that Doctor Dave would work to help addicts kick their habits. Soon the seekers who came here to turn on, tune in, and drop out began arriving at his office at the General for help. Then he leased an old dentist's office in a beat-up yellow Victorian at the corner of Haight and Clayton. On the first day 250 showed up, and then more arrived the next day and the day after that.

In his book about this era in San Francisco, *The Season of the Witch*, David Talbot writes: "A long line of patients in granny

dresses, buckskins and other light clothing stretched around the corner, shivering miserably in the wet fog. . . . By the third day, [the clinic's] stockpiles of bandages, antibiotics, and penicillin were depleted. When clinic doctors ran out of tranquilizers, all they could do was encourage patients freaking out on drugs to concentrate on flickering candles." On the door still is the hand-painted sign from that time: "No dealing. No holding drugs. No using drugs. No alcohol. No pets. Any of these can close the clinic. We love you."

Smith felt these were his people, rejects like his Okie forebears. Patients presented with pneumonia, hepatitis, venereal disease, malnourishment, and ailments from eating food procured in dumpsters. At a meeting at his alma mater, UCSF, he tried to secure support for the venture, declaring famously, "Health care is a right, not a privilege."

Still, he found it hard to get funding for the clinic, and some musicians and their promoters came to the rescue. A check for $25,000 came in from Lou Adler, who organized the 1967 Monterey Pop Festival, and promoter Bill Graham did two concerts at the Fillmore, raising $5,000 each. "I remember running into Janis Joplin and Grace Slick in front of the Fillmore, thanking them, one of them saying, 'Hey, you're a good cause.'"

But it wasn't all peace, love, and understanding. A drug

dealer, apparently unhappy that some of his clients were getting clean with the clinic's help, put a contract out on Smith's life. A friend put Smith in touch with the biker gang, the Hell's Angels, who promised him they'd take care of it. "My life was the guy's insurance policy. I die, he dies. That was the message they gave him. He disappeared."

Eventually, the clinic thrived, and it's here to this day. By one recent count, there are 1,200 modeled on it across the nation. "It was about nonjudgmental care." The we-love-you part on the sign. "The whole specialty of addiction medicine was just starting—there are 7,000 specialists in that now," Smith says, before ruefully adding. "Unfortunately, the drug problem is worse than it was."

1941

OLDEST BIKE SHOP

AMERICAN CYCLERY

510 Frederick St.

Cycling is big in San Francisco, in spite of its dauntingly steep hills or possibly because of them. The nation's second bicycle club, the first on the West Coast, was founded here in 1876, shortly after the bicycle's invention, when the relatively awkward, newfangled machines were known as high-wheelers, penny farthings, and bone-shakers. Shortly after their local introduction, a writer for the *San Francisco Chronicle* enthused: "Why should he go afoot, while he can ride a mustang of steel, who knows his rider and never needs a lasso?"

From 1941 on, one of the seats of bike culture in San Francisco has been American Cyclery, a store founded by a bike racer. Oscar Juner was a Jersey Boy (from Newark) who settled out West after a successful career of cycling in velodromes around the continent. In these popular races, Juner competed as one of two teammates against another duo over six days, once helping to fill Madison Square Garden. His biggest victory came in the late 1930s in Los Angeles, in the city where he once famously snagged the hat of a front-row fan, Hollywood star Bette Davis. Giddy times, but tough ones were to come: the German American Juner served in the US military in the fight against the country of his ancestors, winning a Purple Heart.

When he started American Cyclery, it was one of several stores in this part of the city, which for a time became Bicycle Central;

now, it's the last one left. One of Juner's old jerseys hangs in a glass case on the wall—it looks like something Captain America might have worn. After he retired from racing, he mentored younger riders at the local, state, and international levels. "He was big on passing along what he knew," says Bradley Woehl, its owner for the last 25 years.

Downstairs in the area staffers call the catacomb, are many hanging bikes, some of them coveted by collectors, as well as an archive of cycling magazines, scrapbooks full of old newspaper clippings, and retro ads. Here Woehl has gathered some Lance Armstrong memorabilia. "After the doping issues, so many people—pharmacists and doctors' offices—they had stuff they wanted to sell."

In 1992, San Francisco saw the first mass ride by the up-with-cycling movement that became known as Critical Mass. On the last Friday of each month, hordes of cyclists, many of them riding bikes sourced at American Cyclery, would take over the streets in an event that has since spread to over 300 cities around the world. Movement leaders have sought to push for safer streets for cyclists and to promote the bike as a good means of transport

for commuters—good environmentally, good for health. "We were pretty involved for the first few years of Critical Mass," says Woehl, some of whose current clients are medics and nurses who bike to and from a nearby hospital.

American Cyclery often sees clients who have strong feelings for their bikes—who venerate these trusty steeds deeply. "Some of the collectors hang the bikes on their walls—as pieces of art," Woehl says. In the course of his work, he has seen an exact replica, he says, of one of the bikes used in the cult-favorite biking movie *Breaking Away*.

The late, local hero, actor-comedian Robin Williams, had a big collection of bikes, some of them sourced or fixed up here. "He was a keen rider." Another well-known sometime client has been The Decembrists' bassist Nate Fury, who named the store one of his favorite places in San Francisco in an ad campaign done up by Google.

GOLDEN GATE PARK

1878

OLDEST PUBLIC GREENHOUSE IN CALIFORNIA

CONSERVATORY OF FLOWERS

100 John F. Kennedy Dr.

The author of a history of Golden Gate Park, Christopher Pollock aptly calls the Conservatory of Flowers, "a relic of the Gilded Age." Certainly, a few of the main tycoons who made their money in the Gold Rush and lived on in gilded splendor were involved in getting this building made. James Lick, a piano- and cabinet-maker who made his fortune in real estate, died in 1876, leaving behind him the bulk of the materials from two greenhouse kits. Two railroad barons (Leland Stanford and Charles Crocker) and one sugar king (Claus Spreckels), among others, arranged to purchase them from the estate and present them to the Park Commission, with the state legislature kicking in funds to help put up this fabulous, airy structure.

The oldest building in the park, it's been somewhat accident-prone, with a fire damaging its first dome in 1883, harming some of the exotic plants and ruining the roost of a giant Brazilian parrot. Afterwards, a bigger dome was added—it's now 55 feet high, 56 feet wide, and weighs a whopping 29,000 pounds. Inside, an imperial philodendron vine, called, unoriginally, Phil, has reached towards the roof for about a century. One of his dropped leaves, about four feet in diameter, was recently on display.

One of those who helped tend to Phil was the first woman gardener, Sidney Stein. She didn't get the job at once, having had to ask park superintendent John McLaren several times if she could help. "Can you spade?" he finally asked her.

Long the sole female gardener on staff, Stein's work ethic helped her get appointed Chief Nurseryman and Manager of the Conservatory. She also became something of a local celebrity. It helped that she gave reporters good quotes, moving blithely from speaking about worms and weeds to manicures and dances. She married late—at age 40, to one Neville Rich Sr.—but died young. Her sister gave a celadon green terracotta bench in her memory.

The bench ended up stored away somewhere, but was rediscovered after the Conservatory took another licking, in 1995, from winds off the Pacific clocked at over 100 miles per hour. The tempest ripped many panels off the building, and the restoration cost a cool $25 million, including the cost of strengthening steel rods put inside some of the wonky old wood beams.

Sidney Stein Rich's bench can now be seen in a plant-bedecked grotto in one of the Conservatory's five main rooms. The first room features Phil and other jungle plants, with a piped-in soundtrack of birds, frogs, and monkeys. Another room nurtures plants of the Cloud Forest, putting the visitor at eye-level with the striking

orchids that sometimes live high up the trees. Another room is filled with ponds topped with gigantic Amazon water lilies and often gaudy, insect-eating plants around their edges.

But along with Phil, the most famous botanical residents here are the *Amorphophallus titanum.* These large, weird-looking plants look like they could give the man-eating one in *Little Shop of Horrors* a run for its money. From a base that resembles a big purple, parfait glass, a tall green member protrudes—hence the *phallus* in its Latin name. They smell wretched—like rotting flesh—and so their colloquial name, the Corpse Flower. When they bloom, once every seven to nine years, it's big box office and the Conservatory stays open late. Says Operations Manager, Drew Risner-Davis: "They are critically endangered in the wild—maybe 400 of them in their natural habitat in one part of Sumatra. So we also try to raise awareness about that."

1894

OLDEST PUBLIC JAPANESE GARDEN IN THE US

JAPANESE TEA GARDEN

75 Hagiwara Tea Garden Dr.

This garden began its life as the Japanese Village and Tea Garden concession at the 1894 California Midwinter Fair. Other countries had similar villages, but the most popular concession, the Japanese Tea Garden, was the only one to outlast the fair.

The oldest public Japanese garden in the US was originally designed by artist Toshio Aoki, who emigrated from Yokohama to San Francisco as a young man, landed jobs as an illustrator and cartoonist, and found a gallery to represent him. The owner of this gallery, George Turner Marsh, was an Australian who spoke fluent Japanese and ran a famous Asian art store in Monterey.

Perhaps in part for cross-promotional purposes, Marsh built and operated the concession at the 1894 fair. At the fair's end he retained businessman Makato Hagiwara to look after the garden, and the park's commission confirmed his appointment going forward.

Under Mayor Jim Phelan the city introduced a regulation declaring that those who were ineligible for citizenship could not hold city jobs. This blocked the employment of Asians, and Hagiwara was let go in 1901. Furious, he opened up a competing garden nearby. In 1906, the parks commission asked him to come back, only not as an employee but as a concessionaire. After his death in 1925, his daughter Takano and son-in-law Goro ran the garden.

Courtesy Japanese Tea Garden

The Hagiwaras's luck then turned bad—really bad. One moonlit night in 1934, their son George's wife Aiko dowsed herself in gasoline and burned herself and her 11-month-old baby boy to death in the garden. And after Pearl Harbor the entire family was sent to an internment camp. At this time, the garden's name was changed to the Oriental Tea Garden, Chinese workers brought in, and a Shinto shrine on-site was demolished.

Many of the garden's potted plants, including some small cypresses, had been purchased by the Hagiwaras and were taken by garden designer Samuel Newsom for caretaking. ("He had studied in Japan from 1934 to 1939," garden supervisor Steven Pitsenbarger says, "and was grateful for his time there, how good people were to him.") After the war, the Parks Commission would not have the Hagiwaras back to live on the site and offered them less money to run it.

Instead of returning they auctioned off the tiny trees, some of which can live for centuries. A doctor and his wife, Hugh and Audrey Fraser, bought the collection, willing it back to the garden after they died. The trees now stand in mute tribute to their former owners, the longtime stewards of this place. Another tribute to the Hagiwaras is a small monument near the gates, done by Japanese American artist Ruth Asawa, which has carved frogs crawling over a little boulder.

The garden's fixed elements have asked for some love of late. Termites had gone at the tori, munching on the hinoki cypress wood from which it was built without nails. "Nail-free construction, something developed over centuries in Japan, can be better in an earthquake," Pitsenbarger says. The pagoda's roof had lost its shingles, and the bells that once rang in the wind were gone. The funds were found to restore it and to find new, appropriate bells. At this writing, stone to build new footings for the pagoda had just been delivered from a quarry in Takasago, Japan, with artisans booked to come over from there to carve and install the rock foundation.

Though the Japanese Tea Garden began as a fairground attraction, through the work of the Hagiwaras and many others it has become something more authentic, a long-term ambassador for the culture and a sign of persistence against long odds.

The World War II internment of Japanese Americans hollowed out San Francisco's Japantown (centered at Post St. and Buchanan St.), and then an urban redevelopment project demolished many of its historic buildings. After each, some families and businesses returned and rebuilt.

Today a concrete pagoda occupies a plaza often filled with teens cosplaying their favorite manga characters. Inside an urban mall attached to the plaza are ramen shops and purveyors of onigiri and black sesame–flavored ice cream; stores dedicated to books, stationery, and pottery; and a flower-arranging school.

Across the street in the pedestrianized, outdoor Buchanan Street Mall, are some monumental origami-inspired pieces by sculptor Ruth Asawa. Here is also one of the city's historic hardware stores, Soko (1698 Post St.). Started in 1925 by the Ashizawa family, the store offers the standard North American hardware goods but also retails Japanese ceramics and tools for woodworking and gardening.

1901

OLDEST PUBLIC BOWLING GREEN IN THE US

SAN FRANCISCO LAWN BOWLING CLUB

320 Bowling Green Dr.

It wasn't, admittedly, the worst result of the 1906 earthquake. Still.

From 1901 on, the San Francisco Scottish Bowling Club had grown their grass from seed, trimmed and watered and rolled it to give a worthy pitch for the ancient game. And then the quake came and heaved up and wrinkled the smooth lawn. After that, the cavalry, in town to help out post-quake, allowed their horses to trample the hand-reared grass.

The game, in some form or goes back perhaps to classical Rome, perhaps to medieval Germany. Certainly, it took hold in England and Scotland, where the game was confined to the upper crust, with legislation in Henry VIII's time requiring contestants to have a certain minimum annual income.

On this side of the pond, the game surfaced with the Brits in colonial Jamestown. And, though the Puritans disapproved, New Englanders played it. Evidence for this is the recent discovery in Boston of a buried ball belonging to one Katherine Nanny Naylor, a well-to-do divorcée in the 18th century who probably didn't give a fig for what the Puritans thought.

In San Francisco, as the club's first name suggests, it came to be played through its links to Scotland. The first bowls used at the club were imported from there, and Scottish American park superintendant John McLaren was the club's first vice president. But it's not a snooty, elitist body, as the sport's history might suggest. It offers free lessons to anyone who calls them up, and its membership is diverse, open to all.

The club's current president, the congenial lawyer David Waters, recently gave me and a friend such a lesson, deploying its satisfyingly rich terminology throughout. First your hands are measured—balls vary from 4-13/16 inches to 5-1/8 inches. Then you're set up at one end of an alley—a 20-foot wide strip of the green, about 120-feet long. The first player bowls out the jack, the little white ball, and then subsequent players try to get their own balls as near to it as possible, which is difficult because the weighted balls curve as they roll. A team's skip stands near the jack and shares pointers by hand signals to the bowler. When my friend accidentally hits the jack with her ball, we learn that this can be a canny strategy to change the game utterly midstream. Other terms we hear include the draw, weight, forehand, backhand, shot bowl, toucher, and, perhaps my favorite, the hog line.

Waters estimates the average age of members to be in their 60s, but they have players in their 90s, and accept anyone over 12. The sport's governing body, Bowls USA, released this paean: "It is a science, the study of lifetime. It is a contest calling for courage, skill, strategy and self-control. It is a test of temper, a trial of honor and a revealer of character."

This makes me feel lousy after a bad showing the first time out.

Never mind. I was heartened to read a local news piece about grandmother Christine Raher who, never having won a trophy in her life, recently took home Woman Bowler of the Year a mere eight years after taking up the sport. Her son, a former varsity basketball player at Cal, was so excited that he supplemented the certificate the club gave her with a big trophy. "At your age, there aren't many athletic activities where you can place first," he reportedly said.

1853

OLDEST SCIENTIFIC INSTITUTION

CALIFORNIA ACADEMY OF SCIENCES

55 Music Concourse Dr.

The first scientific institution west of the Mississippi was founded by seven amateurs, men wanting to make "a thorough, systematic survey of every portion of the State and the collection of a cabinet of her rare and rich productions." A purple bit of prose, but the goal has been achieved, and then some: The museum now holds 46 million specimens from California, the Asia-Pacific region, and points beyond.

In addition to making artful use of these specimens to tell some of the stories of life on this planet, the new building, completed in 2008, now houses state-of-the-art teaching aids, including an aquarium, planetarium, and a captive rainforest. It also employs about 100 working scientists. Some of these recently identified 300 new species of plant and animal on a research trip to the Philippines; others can get called to the coast to figure out the cause of death when a whale washes ashore.

The Academy of Sciences's green roof

Not bad for an organization founded by men who mainly did natural science as a hobby. Several of the founders were trained as medical doctors, and one worked as a pharmacist. One of the more remarkable of the trained medics who became associated with the institution in its first half century was a German immigrant named Hans Hermann Behr, a disciple of the globetrotting scientist Alexander von Humboldt. A founding member of the forest-bathing Bohemian Club, the polyglot was, alas, correct in predicting the extinction of the Xerces Blue, a butterfly that once flitted about the oceanside dunes of South San Francisco and gave its name to the insect-protecting organziation, the Xerces Society.

By the 1870s, crowds of 80,000 per annum were coming to the Academy's museum, located in what is now Chinatown, to see its exhibits, especially its excavated wooly mammoths. In 1891, the growing institution moved into a home on Market Street, but it burned down after the 1906 quake. As luck would have it, an expedition to the Galapagos had not yet returned to the city with its haul. When it did, it would form the nucleus of the Academy's present-day collection. An additional small save: As the fire moved towards the building, staff botanist Alice Eastwood reportedly rushed in, saving over 1,200 of her plants. She also helped convince her friend, John McLaren, then the superintendent of Golden Gate Park, to look favorably on the Academy's post-quake plans to rebuild there.

Visitors to the current building—the work of Italian star architect Renzo Piano—tend first to make a pilgrimage to see the albino alligator Claude in his mock bayou opposite the main entry. He's become something of a mascot for the Academy since he arrived in 2008; the whiteness of these rare creatures tends to make them targets in the wild. Efforts to provide him with alligator companionship failed, though, after former cage-mate Bonnie bit him, requiring the amputation of one of the fingers on his right claw.

The Senior Director of the Steinhart Aquarium, Bart Shepherd, numbers off several other aquatic beasts worth tracking down: a rare peppermint angelfish (electric orange with white stripes), a crew of African penguins, an octopus ("they're so smart," Shepherd says, "we sometimes give them puzzles to solve"), and what he says is "perhaps the oldest fish in a public aquarium in the world", the Australian lungfish Methuselah, who is probably close to 100 years old.

Just behind the Academy is the AIDS Memorial Grove (Nancy Pelosi Drive and Bowling Green Drive), the nation's first monument to that earlier pandemic. Conceived in the thick of the first wave of the North American crisis, the memorial had its groundbreaking in 1992. The names of some of those who died are carved into a series of benches, on rocks in a creek bed, and in a stone circle that is the centerpiece of the redwood- and rhododendron-filled dell. Marked here are the deaths of Steve Silver, founder of the local satiric revue Beach Blanket Babylon, and the San Francisco-based pop star Sylvester. But it's the heartfelt tributes to less famous people that hit me each time: "In fun–loving memory, Allen B. Miller;" "Stephen J. Bathurst . . . Your joy sparkled," and a round rock with just "Norman" carved into it.

1898

OLDEST MODEL BOAT CLUB

SAN FRANCISCO MODEL YACHT CLUB

1217 John F. Kennedy Dr.

Christopher Guest should make a movie about these people. The man who's directed films showing the offbeat passion of dog-show fanatics and small-town theatre troupers would surely get a kick out of the members of this club, the oldest of its kind in America. "There is a keen interest in the Dickie Cup," a profile in the magazine *Model Yachting* says of one of the many competitions run here. Its winner gets to fly a miniature blue pennant until the next year's race. If you're beaten in the Dickie, though, there are also the Virgil, Lyon, Moyes, and Tofte Cups, as well as the prestigious George Doyle Championship regatta race. Over the years, the magazine profile states, roped-off areas have sometimes proved necessary to curb crowd enthusiasm.

"The competition can get so fierce on race day," says Commodore Rob Weaver. "To give you some idea, after 50 races last season, I lost by one point." Still tasting the bitterness of this loss, he repeats, "By one point."

Weaver is a longtime former "big-boat sailor" (as regular yachtsman are called in this sphere where all is miniaturized) and works as a lawyer during the week. Come the weekend during race season, as often as not, he's out here on Spreckels Lake near the Pacific end of Golden Gate Park. He might have his 70-inch yacht *Chinese Algebra* competing in the Santa Barbara class or his 54-inch *Res Ipsa* giving its all in the Infinity 54 category. It might be a day for his 45-inch *Angry Crow* to compete (this is the one that barely, barely lost last year) or his 39-inch *Goose* (in the Odom class).

Some of the yachts you'll see here are guided by remote controls, and others sail with some pre-electric mechanisms trimming the sails. These can have a vane set up near the stern that responds to the wind and moves the rudder accordingly or an attachment to the mainsail that also shifts the rudder when the wind shifts. Other clubs have moved entirely to radio-controlled craft, but the SFMYC has kept the faith with its fleet of so-called free sailors.

The craftsmanship is often extraordinary. Here are boats rigged with little jibs, mainsails, batwings, top sails, and bowsprits, with ropes tied into positively picayune versions of the correct knots. Many of the club's most legendary boats came out of collaborations between members with different skillsets: a retired painter and carpenter; a jeweler (who did the tiny metalwork); an engineer (who designed mini steam, gas, and diesel engines for the so-called stinkpots); and a naval architect.

"Some of our members are here for the craftsmanship, to enjoy it and maybe to build their own," says Weaver. A fixer-upper can cost as little as $200, a kit boat about $500, and a top-tier Wheeler can sell for $4,500 and up.

"But for others," Weaver says, "it's the thrill of the competition that's the draw."

Race days sometimes have a Dixieland Jazz band giving it all a yesteryear soundtrack. Sometimes rubber duckies are released into the lake to be rounded up by mini-tugs. Other times a raft topped with Barbies is set adrift so the model yachts can rescue the damsels from their distress. Occasionally, small war boats chug about, exchanging fire from their even smaller cannons.

But the races are the thing. With the numbers writ (relatively) large on the sails, sometimes there's some mid-race betting on the outcomes. Occasionally, there are collisions between boats and other missteps requiring that the one in the wrong do a circle or, in the case of graver offenses, two turns, while the rest of the little armada sails on.

Spreckels Lake was filled for the first time with water pumped from an underground aquifer by a windmill put up just after the turn of the 20th century. It's called the Dutch Windmill, and locals often say (falsely) that it came as a gift from Queen Wilhelmina. Actually, it was built and designed locally with funds from the park commission. A couple of years later a companion was erected for it, this one given by banker Samuel G. Murphy, for whom it is named. For many years, the two workhorses, with their thick walls and vast wings, helped green Golden Gate Park. But more efficient electric pumps eventually replaced them, and the pair fell into picturesque disrepair. This wouldn't do. Committees were struck and funds raised, and each has now been gussied up, the sails allowed to harvest the wind on special occasions, as when the running race Bay to Breakers finishes near them.

Castro, the Mission, Potrero Hill, SoMa

1883

OLDEST PRO SPORTS TEAM

SAN FRANCISCO GIANTS

Oracle Park, 24 Willie Mays Plaza

The winningest team in baseball history is not, as is commonly supposed, the New York Yankees, but another team with roots in New York—one known, when it started in 1883, as the Gothams. A couple of years later the team's manager was allegedly so overcome at how well his squad played that he called them "his big fellows, his giants"—and the second name stuck. When the Giants moved to San Francisco from New York in 1958, another pro sports team, the 49ers, was already here. But with its 2014 move to a new stadium nearer to San Jose, the Giants took over the title of the city's oldest pro sports team—the oldest by virtue of its founding, the oldest one still here in the city proper.

These are not, of course, the titles that matter. The Giants have eight World Series wins, most of them before the team's midcentury move west. When it arrived, the team brought great expectations with them—and a famous hex put on it by New Yorkers upset by the move. It took a whopping 52 years to retire the so-called Curse of Coogan's Bluff, with the relocated Giants finally winning the World Series for the first time since the move in 2010.

Alfonso Felder, an executive VP with the team, says: "That win was this great coming together—a new stadium, the team a band of eccentric, diverse characters, something made all the more powerful by the long wait.

“That was my first job, in high school, as an usher there,” he goes on. “I got to hang out with the older guys who'd been ushers with the team from the start in San Francisco.” Felder was there the famous day in 1989, when the Loma Prieta earthquake hit midway through a World Series fought against the Oakland A's. “I was upstairs [in Candlestick Park] and felt the building shake. Because of a lock on the entry gates, some parking issues, there was a limited ability to get out.” To add insult to injury, Oakland ultimately swept the series.

For five decades, this was the team's story. Notwithstanding its many star players, it never quite came together for them after the move. The great Willie Mays helped the team win the National

Courtesy S.F. Giants

League pennant in 1962, knocking out the Los Angeles Dodgers, but they faltered against the Yankees in the World Series. The team's great star in the 1990s and early 2000s, Barry Bonds, helped propel them to the 2002 World Series, but they again came up short against the Anaheim Angels. The discovery of Bonds's steroid use also cast a pall over that era. During this long drought, there was periodic talk of moving the team on to Toronto or Tampa Bay, or even shuffling it off to Buffalo.

But near the turn of the millennium, new owners had a different idea, helping Felder and the executive team build the first privately funded urban stadium in nearly 40 years. Since its completion, it has had many names, but it's now called Oracle Park. More consistent has been the quality of play. The team that put the curse to rest had no single star, but several—a superlative bullpen and starting pitchers Tim Lincecum, Madison Bumgarner, and Matty Cain sending pitches towards a stalwart catcher, Buster Posey. Two years later, in 2012, they'd win the World Series again . . . and again in 2014. They've often been in contention since then.

Today, new traditions have been born. Behind the name-shifting stadium is a little body of water, a spit off the bay that's been rechristened McCovey Cove for longtime first baseman Willie McCovey, and a home run that reaches it is called a splash hit.

1791

OLDEST BUILDING

MISSION SAN FRANCISCO DE ASIS, AKA MISSION DOLORES

3321 16th St.

In the late 18th century the great powers of Europe jockeyed for position in the Americas: Spain claimed dominion over California but worried about Russian incursions from the north. So the Viceroy of New Spain sent an expedition of priests and soldiers northward, led by one Captain Juan Batista de Anza. They celebrated an outdoor mass near the site of this adobe mission in 1776. Named for the animal-loving, voluntarily poor saint who'd give the city his name, the mission's informal title came from a stream spotted on, and named for, Good Friday, or Viernes de Dolores, Spanish for the Day of the Sorrows.

And sorrows came. In the nearly 50 years that it operated, the mission didn't achieve its goal of founding a Christian Utopia. The idea was to baptize local natives into their faith and teach them the basics of farming and animal husbandry. Then, after a decade, they would help set them up in small agricultural homesteads run by Catholic rules.

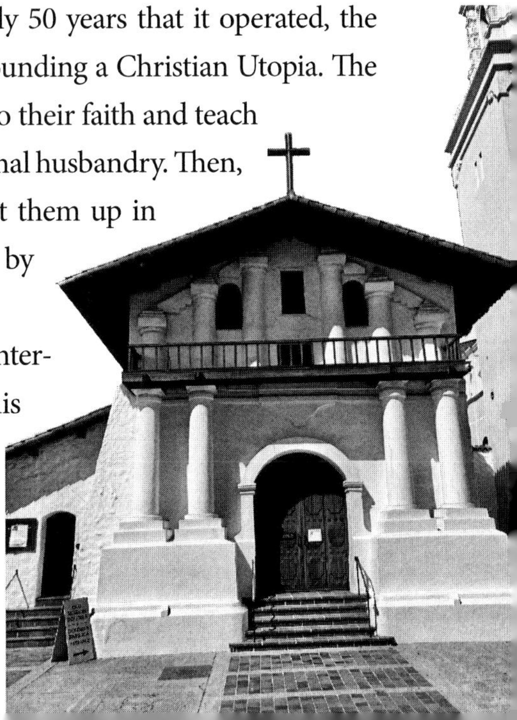

But the members of the hunter-gatherer tribes that occupied this territory—now loosely grouped under the rubric the Ohlone—had their own ways. Malcolm

Margolin, in his seminal book *The Ohlone Way*, details local beliefs about creation (the gods Coyote, Eagle, and Hummingbird presided), courtship (highly formalized), marriage (which could end in divorce), and homosexuality (accepted). The tribes drew year-round sustenance from the area by hunting deer and waterfowl, making flour from acorns, and digging up shellfish on the beaches of the Bay and Pacific.

By persuasion and coercion, the priests brought natives into the Mission. They separated men and women into dorms, gave them new names and clothes, and required that they work at building and maintaining the church and its campus as well as growing crops. Completed in 1891 with 36,000 adobe bricks, the mission mainly speaks of Catholic tradition, with fine painted sculptures of saints and depictions of Christ's passion. The magnificent, saint-filled reredos at the mission's altar stands in front of a mural that features the pierced hearts of sacred figures. But the mark of the native workers is here, too. They formed the mission's distinctive roof tiles by curving red clay over their thighs and shins.

The recently canonized head of the California missions during their early years, Junípero Serra, preached here at least once. Margolin writes that "he carried with him a chain with which he repeatedly beat himself before congregations of awestruck Indians." Local historian Gary Kamiya writes that priests sometimes punished native women who miscarried by ordering them beaten and put in the stocks and then forcing them to carry around a red wooden doll representing the dead child. Natives periodically fled—in 1796, 200 of 872 ran off—but they were often pursued and brought back.

When Mexico declared its independence from Spain in 1821, it took California with it and began to phase out the mission project, leaving Mission Dolores to function as a parish church. In the

American period, the missions Spain established throughout the state fell into decrepitude, with periodic revivals of interest in them as survivors of an earlier era.

In a room behind the church proper are plaques, maps, and artifacts speaking of the precontact life. Under glass are a duck decoy made of tule (to aid in hunting), a ball (used in a native game that resembles soccer), and ceremonial feathered headdresses (recreated based on a visiting artist's painting). In a city with so few physical reminders of the area's first inhabitants, this room gives at least a few specifics. The mission's exhibit curator Jonathan Galvan is a descendant of natives drawn into the mission system.

Attached to the Mission is the city's oldest cemetery. It is also one of the top tourist draws here, in part for its antiquity, in part because it played a key role in Alfred Hitchcock's 1958 film Vertigo. *The movie features a young Kim Novak wandering through the graveyard, then standing before the grave of her character's supposed Spanish ancestor, Carlotta Valdes. The film's climactic scene is set in a Mission (one down in San Juan Batista), with James Stewart, suffering from a fear of heights, struggling to climb its bell tower.*

A statue of priest Junípero Serra has a place here, as does another of a Mohwonk maiden. Approximately 5,000 Ohlone natives are buried here or hereabouts in unmarked graves. In recent years a circular clearing has been added in further remembrance, with a traditional dome-shaped reed house—as if to give them a home they would recognize.

1960s

OLDEST MISSION BURRITO

EL FARO AND TACQUERIA LA CUMBRE

2399 Folsom St., 515 Valencia St.

There is agreement on one thing: The first Mission burrito was made in late September sometime in the 1960s. From there, the two main origin stories, both plausible enough, diverge.

At El Faro (2399 Folsom St.), owner Febronio Ontiveros claimed he first prepped the iconic dish on September 26, 1961, adapting a meal that the immigrant from Durango, Mexico, had eaten when working the fields in California's Central Valley. Some hungry firefighters presented at his Mexican-American eatery, and he used two flour tortillas together to contain the elements of the burrito that conquered San Francisco. Only later would the supersized tortillas needed to wrap these big burritos become widely available.

Near the other edge of the Mission is the other contender: Tacqueria La Cumbrae (515 Valencia St.). This was once a butcher store owned by Raul and Micaela Duran, also Mexican immigrants. They introduced the overstuffed wraps as a side offering in their meat store—it was Micaela's idea of a good meal for a working person, with all the main food groups represented. They were so popular that the Durans turned the space into a restaurant and started to serve them on September 29, 1969—a date they remembered well, since it was Micaela's birthday. They rest their case in part on a claim that the couple got a musical high school student, one Jorge Santana, to make the necessary big flour tortillas. Jorge was the brother of Carlos, and would go on to become a singer. These doughy wraps are a key part of the Mission Burrito. They weren't available anywhere else, according to the couple, so no one else could have been making a Mission Burrito until the Santana kid started.

Food historians have tended to side with El Faro. But both taquerias have certainly played a role in popularizing the dish, helping it go from local delicacy to global phenomenon.

Generally 10 inches long and 3 inches in diameter, these wraps depart from the Mexican originals in having rice and beans (pinto, black, or refried) in them. The meat can be carne asada (citrus-marinaded grilled beef strips), al pastor (pork seasoned with pineapple and chili), or pollo verde (chicken cooked in salsa verde), to name three popular fillings. Then often, there's cut avocado or guacamole, Mexican crema, cheese (usually Jack), and some chopped cilantro.

Locals play with the basic recipe. *New Yorker* writer Calvin Trillin once said of the San Francisco burrito that it "has been refined and embellished in much the same way that pizza has been refined and embellished in Chicago." These days you can find vegan burritos (with grilled squash, mushrooms, or tofu), fancy ones (with duck confit or venison), and ones filled with grilled seafood.

Within San Francisco there are, by one recent count, over 150 taquerias and taco trucks that serve the Mission burrito—the word is Spanish for "little donkey," since, like those beasts of burden, burritos also tend to get loaded up. And they're so wrapped up in the civic ethos that locals wax poetic about them. For some, they embody an idea of what San Francisco should be, even what the US should strive for. The owner of (the excellent) Papalote (3409 24th St.), Victor Escobedo, recently told broadcaster Kristee Ono, "People say America should be a melting pot. I say it should be a burrito. There's the black beans, the rice. It doesn't all go in the blender. All the elements are separate but they come together."

OLDEST ICE CREAM PARLOR, SODA FOUNTAIN, AND LUNCH COUNTER

ST. FRANCIS FOUNTAIN

2801 24th St.

There have been changes made to the St. Francis Fountain over the years, of course. But it doesn't feel that way. The lunch counter at 24th and York was started in 1918 by an immigrant from Sparta, Greece, James Christakes, who lived in an apartment above. Born into that apartment in the 1920s, his son Chris worked in the restaurant his whole life and passed it to Peter and James, his sons.

The restaurant accrued functions over the years, moving from luncheonette serving the neighborhood's working-class clientele to candy-maker (fudge, marshmallows, peanut brittle) to ice-cream fountain (it made both the sodas and ice cream for floats). The interior remains pretty close to the remodel Chris did at mid-century, though the glass floor tiles and curved glass candy case date from his father's time.

Chris helped run the joint from his childhood on, and once told the *New York Times*: "I knew I'd never starve in this business. Ice cream is eternal." Certainly, sometimes the making of it must have seemed endless, with staff producing 800 gallons per month.

The old Bay-Area brands are honored here, with a coffee can from Hills Brothers holding some pens and a soap holder from Borax in the washroom. Space is at a premium in the tight restaurant, but the new owners left an old phone booth in one corner, with a defunct rotary-dial pay phone in it.

Two longtimers in the restaurant industry, Peter Hood and Levon Kazarian, bought the place in 2002, the Christakes family having sold it two years earlier. Its interim owner almost closed it—the corner had become a hang-out for drug-dealers, and sales were down. But Hood and Kazarian soldiered through.

The candy-making lore went away with the Christakeses, so the glass case is now filled with Good 'n' Plenty, baseball cards, Duran Duran cards, and peanut-butter taffy. The ice-cream machines were on their last legs, so they decided to source from another legacy Mission business, Mitchell's (see sidebar below).

After giving the restaurant a good deep clean, the new owners expanded the kitchen and the menu offerings. On the counter there's another Bay Area OG product, Heinz ketchup, and next to it is some salsa picante. There are taquerias and botanicas all around St. Francis now, so huevos rancheros and chili are on offer here. It also has some vegan fare.

But the pièce de resistance is now—and ever shall be—a vanilla malted, the shake coming to the table in a fluted, stemmed glass, with whipped cream and (if you're lucky) a cherry on top. The glass is as cold as its contents, and there's a long spoon next to it for scooping out remnants.

Local food writer Nico Madrigal-Yankowski grew up near the St. Francis and recently wrote about a lunch there with his mother in SFGATE. He was moved by the old sign that you see as you exit, "The St. Francis Fountain Thanks You." By way of valediction, he writes: "Whether it was the original owners who set up shop more than a century ago or Levon Kazarian and Peter Hood who own it now, St. Francis Fountain has always been, and will always be, a labor of love."

Kazarian and Hood have recently put the restaurant on the market for $350,000, Kazarian to go run a place in Joshua Tree, Hood to retire.

St. Francis's ice cream supplier is Mitchell's (688 San Jose Ave.). Founded in 1953 by two brothers, it's likely the oldest ice-cream maker still based in the city (The ice cream sandwich specialist IT'S-IT started in 1928 but has relocated to Burlingame.)

With their roots in dairy farming, the Mitchells started by offering rich ice cream—16 percent buttercream when 14 percent is standard. In the 1960s they went tropical with mango and moved into ube (aka purple yam), langka (jackfruit), and buko (young coconut). These are flavors popular with Filipino-Americans, many of whom have settled in the nearby Excelsior.

The shop's other flavors also reflect a diverse customer base, including Mexican Chocolate (the chocolate sourced from Guittard), Horchata (for the rice-derived cinnamon drink popular in Mexico), Café Serré (Vietnamese coffee flavor), and Thai Tea. And there's an ice-cream flavored with that fruit widely associated with California, the Avocado.

1913

OLDEST MOVIE THEATER

THE ROXIE

3117 16th St.

"The Roxie has had more lives than a cat," says Lex Sloan, the executive director of the nonprofit that owns and runs the cinema. "It has nearly died many times."

And it has also had many names. It was founded under the name The Poppy by a jeweler with a handle out of Raymond Chandler. Philip H. Doll had a yen for show business, but not much knack, and seems to have fled town to duck out on the theater's creditors. The 300-seat movie house then became the New 16th Street, the Rex, the Gem, the Gaiety, and finally, in 1933, the Roxie—probably after New York's grand movie palace, the Roxy with a "y," which opened in 1927.

Some time in its early years it acquired a Deco marquee from a car dealership in Oakland, to which it added a neon version of its name. Unusually, there is no space on the sign above the door to list the movies it is showing. "It was then—and is now—this neighborhood place where people walk by, check out the film, and then maybe come in," Sloan says.

The films in its first couple of decades were silents, and then it (and the pictures) got sound. As the *Chronicle*'s longtime film critic Mick LaSalle once wrote: "This is the theater where San Franciscans long gone went to see two-reelers, discovered Charlie Chaplin and Mary Pickford, and, later, Clark Gable and Bette Davis."

But the Roxie was never a place for glam releases. That was left to the likes of the Castro, built in 1922 a few blocks away. The Roxie's showing space is plain, just Deco asparagus bunch lamps on the wall for ornamentation. In the 1950s and '60s, it got second- and third-run movies. "When we did a recent renovation," Sloan says, "we found a film projectionist's notes in the walls, saying that, before the feature, he played cartoons, *Jeopardy*, and the news. It also had a note saying, 'Did you pay the phone bill?'"

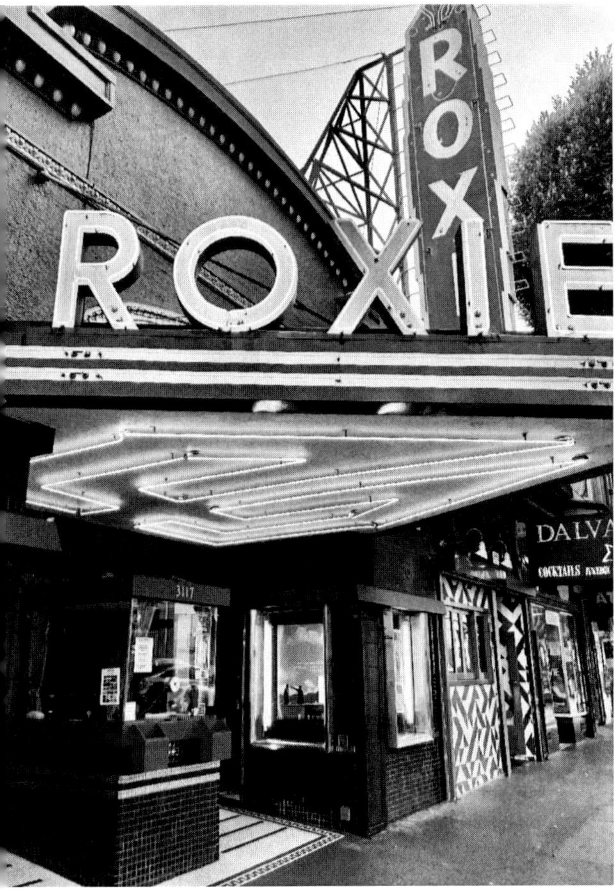

In addition to showing films, the hall has hosted bingo nights, Sloan says. It fell on hard times in the 1970s, and paid its bills by showing blue movies. In 1975 a small group of film lovers got together and proposed to reinvent it as a place showing risky foreign films. In 1979, it hosted the US premiere of Luis Buñuel's *L'Age d'Or*, a sexy, surrealist work long banned in the US.

It hasn't always been easy to make a go of it playing niche films. In the early aughts the Roxie got a rescue from a local college, which used it to screen videos for its media studies program. The college went out of business, and then in 2009 the theater registered as a nonprofit. It certainly took its new status literally in its first few years, not profiting.

But in 2015 its film-loving board of directors resolved to raise enough money to put the Roxie on solid footing. And they and their staff, Sloan included, have done so, securing support from arts foundations and the city.

The big theater and its 50-seater next door, The Little Roxie, have helped incubate many small film festivals, and the complex often serves as one of the host venues for the main San Francisco Film Festival. Funders recently donated enough to do the delicate work needed to restore the neon-lit marquee.

The theatre closed for 433 days during COVID, but "we made it through," Sloan says. "We hope to remain a place that screens the weird and wacky stuff, the stuff you'll see nowhere else."

Just a few blocks east of the Roxie is San Francisco's oldest live theater. The 480-seat Victoria (2961 16th St.) began its life in 1908 as Brown's Opera House. The Brown in question was Edmund Brown, whose son Pat and grandson Jerry both became governors of California. Put up to handle touring vaudeville shows—Mae West played here—it had to change it up when vaudeville died. For years it programmed also-ran movies, giving away Depression glassware as a promotion in the 1930s. In the 1960s it became a burlesque house, with the likes of Blaze Starr, Tempest Storm, and Virginia "Ding Dong" Bell on stage. Since then it's become a rental for different troupes. The historic building needs a deep-pocketed patron or a dynamic in-house repertory company to make a real go of it.

1939

OLDEST BODY SHOP

ALIOTO'S GARAGE

1835 Folsom St.

When you search online for Alioto and San Francisco, the storied family restaurant on Fisherman's Wharf, Alioto's, comes up, as does the city's former mayor Joseph Alioto.

"We're not them," Matthew Alioto says, "though I guess, we're all from Sicily originally. The mayor gave me a coin when I was born and, at the restaurant on Fisherman's Wharf, they're always good to us."

Matthew and his brother Christopher are the third generation to run the city's oldest auto-body shop. It was founded by their grandfather Frank "Babe" Alioto, the first American-born son of immigrants from the aforementioned Sicily. The cars Babe fixed included Packards, Chryslers, and Plymouths, and he soon brought his son, Frank Jr., into the business.

Babe and Frank Jr. worked hard together and fought often, by Matthew's account. "The stories I heard growing up were of my Dad, Frank Jr., storming out of the shop, saying he'd never return, and then sitting down over a family pasta dinner with his dad, and returning to work the next day."

Babe died young, and Frank Jr. had to shoulder the business and become the family's main breadwinner at the age of 22. His widowed mother would take a bus across the city to bring him his lunch. When he was courting the woman who'd become his wife, an airline stewardess named Carolyn, he once looked pensively

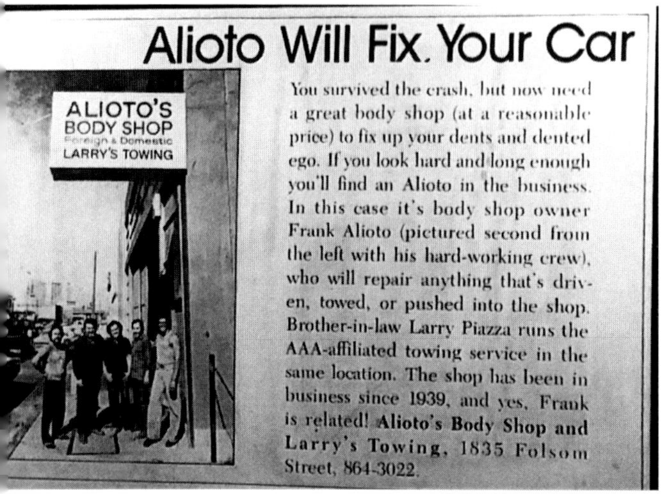

Alioto Will Fix. Your Car

You survived the crash, but now need a great body shop (at a reasonable price) to fix up your dents and dented ego. If you look hard and long enough you'll find an Alioto in the business. In this case it's body shop owner Frank Alioto (pictured second from the left with his hard-working crew), who will repair anything that's driven, towed, or pushed into the shop. Brother-in-law Larry Piazza runs the AAA-affiliated towing service in the same location. The shop has been in business since 1939, and yes, Frank is related! **Alioto's Body Shop and Larry's Towing, 1835 Folsom Street, 864-3022.**

out the window into the rain. His date suspected he was thinking romantic thoughts, but no. He reportedly told her, "All this rain means there are going to be lots of cars to fix."

Frank Jr. ran the shop from the early 1960s to shortly before his death in 2014, growing the business to nearly its current size of four locations, three in the city and one in San Mateo. "His body gave out," Matthew said. "It had been in harm's way so often, run over by a tow-truck once—but his mind, it was there. And always focused on the shop."

Each Christmas Alioto's main shop on Folsom, would be done up in a theme—a Hawaiian luau, a Fajita bar. "There was always a wooden dance-floor brought in, several drinks bars," Matthew recalls. "All the benches where we do the work were brought up to table level, with tablecloths and food laid on them. Sometimes a thousand people came, cars double-parked up the whole block, police maybe coming to crack down, but staying for drinks."

Frank Jr.'s sons took over the shop in the late aughts, though both had worked there off and on for years. Armed with a business degree, Christopher manages the increasing number of relationships needed to succeed in this sphere—with the insurers, automakers, and the original equipment manufacturers.

The shop has developed an expertise with Tesla, Porsche, Honda, Subaru, and GM, and relationships with insurers like State Farm.

In the early years of working with Tesla, Matthew remembers a spectacular accident: "One of the first [Tesla] Model X's we got in because a guy was driving down Columbus St. with both its falcon doors open and ran into a sign, totally mangling the car." A single sentence that conjures up the decadence and gadgetry of tech-boom San Francisco.

Both Matthew and Chris have children. Do they see another generation following them into the family business? "It's too early to say," Matthew says. "Who knows what they'll want? Anyway, the business is changing so quickly—maybe soon, fixing cars will be more like fixing an iPhone." One thing that hasn't changed though: When it rains in San Francisco, Alioto's gets busy.

1896

OLDEST BREWERY

ANCHOR BREWING COMPANY

1705 Mariposa St.

Anchor came out of an earlier brewery started by Gottlieb Brekle, a German immigrant who came here in the Gold Rush. It was in 1871 that Brekle started running Anchor's predecessor brewery out of a saloon in Russian Hill, and the brewery took the name Anchor in 1896—the official year of founding.

Anchor was one of many breweries in those pre-refrigeration days to air-cool the mash, the so-called wort, that came out of the brewing kettles. The practice was to leave this mixture to cool and ferment further in rooftop baths, and clouds of steam would billow off these into the cold, early morning air. This is, anyway, one story of how Anchor's most famous brew came to be called Steam Beer. But some say a San Franciscan named Pete Steam pioneered it; others that it was an adjective given out willy-nilly in the steam era to speak to something's coolness and power. Whatever the case, Anchor was the only San Francisco brewery after the advent of mass refrigeration to continue with this method of brewing.

The history section of Anchor's website uses local author Daniel Handler's title: An Unfortunate Series of Events—and it's an apt way to think of the brewery's checkered past. Towards the end of the 19th century Brekle passed the brewery along to two fellow German Americans, Ernst F. Baruth and his son-in-law Otto Schinkel Jr. So far, so good.

Fritz Maytag and Anchor's staff

The unfortunate series began with Baruth's sudden death in 1906 and continued with that year's big quake. The post-quake fire consumed the factory and then, just a year later, Schinkel was knocked down by a streetcar and died. Under new management, it limped into the 1920s, only to be shut down (at least officially) by Prohibition. Just when Prohibition ended and Anchor could begin brewing openly again, another fire destroyed its factory.

Again, it picked itself up, finding new premises not far from its current digs in Potrero Hill. At the mid-century, the American craze for the watery lagers produced by the mega-breweries hit San Francisco. Still, even if they couldn't beat 'em, they decided not to join 'em. Says its current Assistant Brewmaster, Tom Riley, "They were crazy people, staying loyal to this idea of brewing from the Gold-Rush days."

But by the mid-1960s the brewery was flirting with bankruptcy, and a young Stanford graduate named Frederick Louis Maytag III—one of the appliance-making Maytags—supposedly learned of its

difficulties one evening while drinking Anchor Steam and bought it for a few thousand dollars. In 1977 he moved the firm into its current home, an old coffee factory in Potrero Hill. Under Maytag, Anchor never aimed to produce for the mass market: "The idea isn't to grow big," he would say, "it's to make good beer consistently." And so, he is often credited with starting the ongoing microbrewery movement.

In 2010, Maytag finally sold out to the California liquor company that also owned Skyy Vodka, and it, in turn, sold Anchor to Japan's Sapporo Holdings Ltd in 2017. Since then Anchor's offerings have expanded to include, at various times, a brown brew named for founder Brekle and an experimental beer following a recipe out of ancient Sumer, named for that Mesopotamian culture's Goddess of Beer.

Maybe it was this offering to the ancient goddess that has helped Anchor see out this long series of unfortunate events. Maybe not. But see it out it did. A selection of Anchor's brews is available at a congenial beer garden and airy taproom just downhill from the factory (495 De Haro St.).

1899

OLDEST MATTRESS MAKER

MCROSKEY MATTRESS CO.

1687 Market St.

They've been called the Rolls-Royce of mattresses, the tufted McRoskeys manufactured and sold from a four-story building on Market Street about a half-mile from City Hall. Built in 1925, the family firm's headquarters are fronted with big windows and "Edward McRoskey Mattress Co." spelled out in gilt letters. On its first and second floors it has airy, bed-filled showrooms, but it becomes something of a rabbit warren up top, with passages and staircases, pipes and ducts going this way and that.

Walking through this is Edward's granddaughter, Robin McRoskey Azevedo, the company's head from 1990 on. Though a sensible businesswoman in no-nonsense shoes, Azevedo is hearing things and seeing things, things that aren't in the here and now. She points down a stairwell. "At closing time, at the end of their shift, you could hear the men all clomping down the stairs, heading for home." She closes her eyes. "Also, there was this whooshing sound the mattresses would make when they slid it down this chute."

The business's history and the city's are, in small ways and large, intertwined. The company was founded by the aforementioned Edward and his brother Leonard, who came here from Chicago, and sold curled hair, tickings, feathers, and silk floss to upholsterers and bedmakers for a few years. They then got into the mattress-making business themselves, in time to profit from the 1906 quake.

For reasons that are still not entirely clear, the two brothers squabbled, parted company, and set up competing businesses in around 1920—which is why there's just Edward's name on the building. After Leonard's death in 1929, Edward had the name and its reputation to himself and firmed up his niche at the luxury end of the bed market with a patent for a tufting machine. "Tufting is taking a piece of string or strong twine through the top and bottom of the mattress," Azevedo says, "to keep the filling material from drifting around." For the most part, McRoskey mattresses still have the distinctive dimpled shape created by tufting. Asked to contrast her firm's mattresses with those sold for crazy low prices online, she says, simply, "Our mattresses are not things you leave behind when you move."

Prospective bed-buyers are encouraged to try the beds on their sides, their backs. "A good sleep is necessary to a good, productive life," Azevedo says. Certainly, some of its customers over the years have been famously productive people: the writer and activist Gloria Steinem and former Secretary of State George Shultz. The company has been deft in marketing its high-end product over the years. Recent ads have featured tattooed sleepers as well as a pair of women and an interracial couple going to bed. "A woman I know said to me about the two women, did I think a company like McRoskey should be doing that?"

Azevedo says. "I said, oh, you mean the sisters? Then someone else called and said the women are young. Can't someone feature older lesbians for once?" For a time, they sent a truck out to San Francisco's hinterlands with a mattress in it for people to try. "The truck was a good advertisement."

McRoskey recently sold the manufacturing portion of the business to another old family-run company, Pleasant Mattress, which now makes the beds, to McRoskey's standards, in Fresno.

Toward the end of the interview, Azevedo sums up the company's long-time core value, "Exercise, eating well, sleeping well—that's the tripod of well-being. We can't help you on the first two, but, on the last one, well, we can."

1978

OLDEST RAINBOW FLAG

GLBT HISTORICAL SOCIETY MUSEUM

4127 18th St.

Gilbert Baker was a dreamy youth who came to San Francisco from the midwest to work as a nurse in a military hospital treating those wounded in Vietnam. After getting his honorable discharge in 1972 he stayed in San Francisco, getting to know one of the first openly gay elected officials in North America, City Supervisor Harvey Milk. In the run-up to an early civic celebration of what later would be be called LGBT Pride, Milk asked Baker if he'd design and produce a flag to wave over the United Nations Plaza on the June day set aside for the event—and a fragment of that flag is on display at this storefront museum.

Milk's aide at the time, Cleve Jones, a close friend of Baker's, recalls: "Gilbert was very much a hippie at heart, with long brown hair and a knack for creating complicated and gorgeous costumes, gowns and art." The rainbow felt like the right symbol to Baker, who died in 2017. "From earliest recorded history," Baker once said, "the rainbow was a symbol of hope." Baker also linked it to "Over the Rainbow" from *The Wizard*

of Oz, long adopted by the gay community as an anthem. Often mocked as a boy, he used to joke about his upbringing in Kansas, "Unlike Dorothy, when the tornado came, I ran right for it, saying, 'Take me away.'"

The flag Baker made had eight hand-dyed colors, not the current six, and Baker would number off the meanings of the colors: "Pink was for sex, red for life, orange was healing, yellow sunlight, green nature, turquoise for magic and art, indigo for serenity, violet for spirit."

The flag was a hit from the start. "Raising it up and seeing it there blowing in the wind," he once said, "it just astounded me that people got it, in an instant . . . that it was their flag. That it belonged to all of us. It was the most thrilling moment of my life."

Happy times for Baker, but sad ones were to follow, when, in November of that year, former Supervisor Dan White killed Milk and the city's Mayor George Moscone. It was Jones who found Milk's bloodied body, once telling me in an interview, "We thought it was all over, gay liberation, gay rights. But then, the next evening, Market Street was flooded with people, everyone, illuminated by the light of the candles they were carrying."

And so, not over, not by a long shot. A San Francisco company, Paramount, soon started to make rainbow flags, using the colors it had on hand, dropping the pink and substituting royal blue for the turquoise and indigo. It has since gone around the world.

The fragment of the flag on display here was almost lost. After the flag first flew it was stored for several years in a damp spot, and extensive mildew was the result. Baker reportedly rescued a fragment of it, storing it among his things. "There was interest in it from the Smithsonian," says Charley Beal, president of the Manhattan-based Gilbert Baker Foundation. "But we decided to send it to San Francisco. We felt we had to get it out of the closet, as it were, to get it on display."

This micro-museum has covered the walls around the case containing the flag with shifting exhibits. One featured Del Martin and Phyllis Lyon, who founded the lesbian rights organization the Daughters of Bilitis, in San Francisco in 1955. Martin once memorably said, "We were fighting the church, the couch and the courts"—since homosexuality was widely denounced by religious authorities as a sin, considered a mental disorder by psychiatrists, and punished as a crime.

Just a few steps away from the museum, on Castro Street, is a plaque marking the location of Harvey Milk's camera shop, which doubled as his campaign office (575 Castro St.).

The Twin Peaks mountains that overlook the gayborhood gave their name to Twin Peaks (401 Castro St.), opened in 1935 and the first bar catering mainly to the LGBT community. Just a few steps over is the Castro Theatre (429 Castro St.), a community landmark completed in 1922 to a design by local movie-palace specialist Timothy L. Pflueger. It was here, after waiting in a line that snaked around the block, that I saw Milk, *the 2008 movie with Sean Penn playing the ebullient supervisor.*

A stone's throw away is a hardware store named Cliff's Variety (479 Castro St.). Along with hardware supplies, it sells rainbow flags and Halloween costumes (the area's Halloween tends to be epic).

1948

OLDEST POTTERY

HEATH CERAMICS

Flagship Store: 2900 18th St.; Outlet: Ferry Building, Stall #12

As a child, Edith Kiertzner saw her large, Danish American family lose its farm in Iowa. In the auction of their belongings, no one bought their dainty Haviland china from France. When Edith decided to start making her own ceramics, she wanted to produce something that was as far from Sunday-best porcelain as possible. "I don't like highly stylized things," she said "I like easy, soft shapes on things. Things that are more like a folk dance than a ballet."

And the pottery she would make had these easy, soft shapes, this stylish absence of evident style. She preferred stonewear in earthy colors, its main ornamentation a speckled glaze. "I didn't think the American way of life was that disciplined. People are more easygoing, more humane, less concerned with status."

Such beliefs were in the air when she studied at an arts-oriented teachers' college in Chicago and at a camp in Batavia, Illinois, run by the Works Progress Administration in the Depression. It was at this camp that she met her social-worker husband Brian Heath—whose surname would later be stamped on the bottom of thousands upon thousands of bowls and plates.

During WWII he headed the regional office of the Red Cross in San Francisco. While teaching at a progressive school during the days, Edith studied ceramics at the Art Institute of San Francisco and Berkeley in the evenings. She was that rare pottery student equally interested in the craft of shaping vessels and the chemistry of glazing them. To help her master this craft, Brian made her a potter's wheel powered by a sewing machine and built a kiln in their small apartment.

Not satisfied with the clays she could get commercially, she and her husband spent many weekends clambering down into abandoned quarries and creek-beds until, outside of Sacramento, she found some that felt just so. She also experimented with kilns that heated at a low temperature, bringing out glazes in gentle colors—soft granite blue, misty green, and warm beige.

The resulting pieces won many admirers. In 1944, she had a solo show at the San Francisco Palace of Fine Arts, and a buyer for Gump's purchased her pieces and set her up in a studio in Chinatown. A couple of years later, a wholesaler of tableware also saw something. He not only placed it in department stores like Neiman Marcus and Marshall Field's but loaned her the money to set up a factory in Sausalito.

Her work hit yet another level thanks to Edgar Kaufmann Jr., the department store heir and New York–based Museum of Modern Art curator. He included Heathware in various exhibits in the 1950s of form-fits-function kitchenware and furniture, and it had nods from similarly minded museums across the country.

The glitzy 1980s weren't kind to Heath, and the pottery limped through the next few decades, sometimes barely able to pay its employees. Brian died of a stroke in 2001, and a bereaved Edith's mind began to go. Though she had long resisted the suggestion that the pottery be sold, at last a young couple, Robin Petrovic and Catherine Bailey, came with the right offer at the right time—shortly before Edith's death in 2005.

The pair have kept on many of the staff who carried the aesthetic and techniques in them and moved a major part of the business back to San Francisco, where the pottery was born. In addition to having a stall in the Ferry Building, they have set up a tile factory and attached a tile and pottery showroom in the Mission. These have helped bring new generations of fans to Heath dishes, these deceptively simple, utterly of-California pieces of useable art.

THE SUNSET

OCEAN BEACH

1929

OLDEST ZOO

SAN FRANCISCO ZOO

Sloat Blvd. at the Great Highway

Founded in 1929, the zoo has roots in the 19th century, coming out of a public fascination with the grizzlies that feature on California's flag. In the 1850s James Capen Adams, aka Grizzly Adams, exhibited a pair of bears he'd captured in the Sierras in a basement in the city. In the late 1880s newspaper publisher William Randolph Hearst challenged one of his reporters to find one in the wild—and the resourceful reporter did so, bringing a bear they ultimately called Monarch to San Francisco. Housed for a time in menageries in the Mission and Golden Gate Park, Monarch sired some cubs in captivity, which modern-day zookeepers cite as the start of the in-house breeding programs.

The present zoo owes its existence to Herbert Fleischhacker, an ebullient businessman whose fortune came from paper, electricity, water companies, and a bank. With funds he contributed and helped raise, the zoo acquired the bulk of its grounds, now about 100 acres in the southwest corner of the city.

The zoo's first big attraction was a massive, saltwater swimming pool for humans—the zoo was, for many years, a pleasure ground for people as well as an exhibitor of animals. The neoclassical facade of the house that once stood next to it is all that remains. Among its other human-centric attractions have been a baseball diamond, a miniature steam train, and a circa-1921 merry-go-round.

But these days, the zoo is putting more weight on the animal side of the equation, focusing on their quality of life as well as on education and support for conservation in the wild. Its longtime program fostering bald eagles was a high-profile part of the successful push to bring wild populations of the national bird back from the brink.

Where the zoo's animals long lived in concrete buildings and adjoining pens, it has spent the last two decades shifting them to open-air habitats, often mingling different complementary beasts together. And so, in the 3-acre section planted with flora native to the African Savanna, long-legged ostriches and crowned cranes pace about among giant kudu antelope, zebras, and reticulated giraffes.

Witnessed on a recent visit: an Indian rhino, nuzzling what looked like empty beer kegs; a koala hanging on to a gum tree; a wolverine trotting out to greet its keeper and penguins wobbling

Courtesy San Francisco Zoological Society

Courtesy San Francisco Zoological Society

about their island. "We have a site on the coast, where we take young penguins born here to learn how to swim and fish, basically to become penguins," says the zoo's communications director Nancy Chan.

Over the years, San Francisco's zoo has generated its share of so-called good-news stories, with contests to name baby animals (Cuddles and Puddles are its longtime hippos) and a visit of giant pandas from China. In 2007 the zoo made international headlines for less welcome reasons, when a female Siberian tiger, Tatiana, scaled the walls of her enclosure to attack some youths who were taunting her. She killed one of the three and injured the other two before being shot and killed herself. In 2020 the zoo got a story with a better ending. A few days after the theft of Maki, a ring-tailed lemur, from the zoo, 5-year-old James Trinh told his skeptical teacher he'd seen a lemur in the playground of his South San Francisco school. It turned out he was right, and Maki was reunited with his troop.

1851

OLDEST CHILDREN'S CHARITY

EDGEWOOD CENTER FOR CHILDREN AND FAMILIES

1801 Vicente St.

The oldest children's charity in the West began its life as the San Francisco Orphan Asylum, set up by women connected to the First Presbyterian Church. "Feed my lambs" was the very Christian motto it adopted in its first decade. The charity soon loosened its ties to any one denomination, renaming itself the San Francisco Protestant Orphan Asylum in 1862—children living there tended to call themselves the "PO kids." Run almost exclusively by women for its first century, the organization has shown a remarkable ability to adapt to changing times.

It was started in 1851, when news came of four siblings en route to California (probably from Australia) who'd lost their parents to disease (maybe cholera). The church ladies sprang into action, raising funds by knocking on doors and securing a cottage for their charges in what was then called Happy Valley—now, roughly, SOMA, the South of Market neighborhood. When it outgrew this home, General Henry Halleck, for a time the head of the Union's Civil War effort, loaned them one of his, refusing to accept any rent.

But the women who ran it—the so-called managers—wanted a permanent home for their charges. Eventually they found and purchased a two-block plot on Haight Street in 1854, building a big stone dorm there and hiring a matron, a nurse, and a teacher. Funds came from the state and a who's who of charitable San Franciscans like retailer Levi Strauss, photography pioneer Eadweard Muybridge, and heiress Lillie Coit. All in all, about 3,500 children came through the orphanage in its first half century.

Courtesy Edgewood Center for Children and Families

Though the Haight Street building survived the 1906 quake, it was already creaky and soon needed replacing. The institute sold the land for cash and bought its current campus, 10 acres in the Sunset district, relocating there in 1923. There the Institute built separate cottages on the site, six of them, each with 20 kids and a house mother. They also rebranded themselves as Edgewood for their proximity to the forested park, the Stern Grove.

"When we took the new name [in 1944], we hadn't really been an orphanage for years," says Gregg Biggs, Edgewood's Director of Advancement. "It was often children with one parent who was unable or unwilling to look after them, or what they called then the children of broken homes." By one estimate, only 6 percent of the young residents in 1944 were orphans. In the 1950s, Biggs says, the group began to try to help emotionally disturbed children. Another shift: It was decided in 1957 that men could join the board.

Now funded primarily by government and via a contract with the health management organization Kaiser Permanente,

Edgewood helped pioneer a program called Kinship, that, as its name suggests, tries to find caregivers for kids in trouble within the broader family. This approach has found imitators across the country and abroad, as has a mental-health program that takes youth in crisis out of hospital emergency rooms and into immediate consultation. Another program focuses on youth who have aged out of foster care and need help adjusting to life as independent adults.

"The aim is to keep young people from falling through the gaps in all the other services," Biggs says. "From looking after orphans showing up in the Gold Rush, to today, serving some of the most marginalized youth, the organization has never lost sight of its purpose."

Courtesy Edgewood Center for Children and Families

1937

OLDEST MOTEL

OCEAN PARK MOTEL

2690 46th Ave.

The year 1937 saw several big changes in how Californians got around. A huge chunk of the coastal highway, Route 1, was completed, as was the Golden Gate Bridge. And the city extended the reach of its municipal train system, the Muni, to the Sunset, allowing downtowners to get to the beach more easily.

Someone who saw the opportunities in these big shifts was Larry Smith, who built a motel overlooking the Pacific and called it Ocean Park, constructing it for a relative song, $15,000 then, just under $300,000 in today's money. He retained the architect Conrad Kett, who gave it a streamlined Art-Deco style with nautical accents, portholes for windows, and curvaceous rails like you'd get on a ship deck.

Current co-owner Marc Duffett didn't intend to get into the hospitality business; he had trained as a painter at the prestigious Rhode Island School of Design and paid his bills out here doing house-painting and handiwork for architects. Nor did his wife Vicki, who had worked as a secretary at a UN agency based in Vienna, coming back to her hometown San Francisco to join in its modern dance scene.

Vicki's father Owen Means was a small-time real estate investor who bought the motel in 1977 with the intention of gussying it up and reselling it. But he died that year, along with Vicki's mother. "We decided, almost overnight, to take it over, me doing everything paper-wise, and Marc doing everything else."

One by one, Marc refreshed the suites. He kept their original tiles, and the suites with kitchenettes feature retro, three-burner Magic Chef stoves. The refreshed building won a commendation from the national Art Deco Society in 1987. "I love its character," says Marc, "the curves, the portholes, the human scale."

The area was a rougher one when they first started running the place, and the motel got held up at gunpoint several times. The pair tell stories in a collaborative, he-said-she-said style.

Him: "So this guy comes to the front room of the office—"

Her: "I'm doing yoga next door—"

Him: "And he says he called about a room. I bend down to look

at the bookings, and when I look up there's this chrome-plated magnum pointing at my head. When this happens, you want to know if it's a business thing or if you have a crazy person there. With this guy, it's business. He says he wants the big money, where is the big money? He demands my wallet, and I say, 'I'm a hippie, I have no wallet.'"

Meanwhile, one of the motel's customers, an ex-Israeli army officer, sneaks up on the gunman, only to be followed by the gunman's partner, in a chain right out of Quentin Tarantino movie.

Her: "The gunman comes into the room where I'm in a yoga pose, and I say, 'Who are you?' He wants to know where my purse is, and I say, trying to get him out, 'Oh, I think it must be in the car . . .' "

Him: "But I'm not thinking straight. I say, 'No, I think you left your purse right over here.'"

The pair collapse in laughter.

These days clients tend to be surfers, people who come to walk their dogs on the beach (dogs can stay for a fee), and family members seeing their loved ones at the nearby UCSF Parnassus Hospital. They sometimes have people to stay who are the fourth generation in their family to come here. Marc says, "They remember a postcard in their grandfather's den, or something in a scrapbook."

SOUTHERN SAN FRANCISCO

BAYSHORE, THE EXCELSIOR, WEST PORTAL, BURLINGAME,
ST. FRANCIS WOOD, BERNAL HEIGHTS, DOGPATCH

1880

OLDEST HARDWARE STORE

CENTER HARDWARE

3003 3rd St.

The story of San Francisco's oldest hardware store begins with an Anglo, Peter Smith, but from there it's dominated by German Americans, many of them named Ernest. It is a tale of two hardware stores, one more oriented to big jobs with big clients, the other more of a neighborhood store, working with homeowners to help them fill the cracks in their walls, unclog their plumbing, and retile their bathrooms.

Smith came to the city during the Gold Rush and opened P.A. Smith Hardware and Glass near the corner of 4th and Brannan in about 1880. San Francisco's nearby port was still active, so it supplied hardware and the tools needed to make injured vessels, well, shipshape. This was also the industrial part of the city, so he had plenty of contracts with trade clients. From Smith, the concern went to Heinz Solbach in the 1930s—who renamed it Center—and to the Blanz family in the 1970s.

Courtesy Center Hardware

The other store involved here was Ocean View Hardware, begun in the 1890s and located on a part of Market Street that passed through a residential neighborhood. This is where the Ernests come in. German immigrant Ernest Leinhardt and his half-brother Ernest Gentner ran the store at first, bringing in Gentner's son named (you guessed it) Ernest after he came home from World War II. This Ernest passed it along to his son, named Keith, and then Keith turned around and bought Center from the Blanzes, abandoning the Ocean View name and brand. Then, in due course, his daughter Jamie came into the firm, the fourth generation involved with it.

The store is now located in a 20,000-foot, rust-red building in the Dogpatch, and Jamie Gentner says the approach of those two different stores have remained in the company's DNA. "Whether you need a single lightbulb or are a city contractor who has to source bulbs for the entire Bay Bridge, we have your back."

Gentner started working at the store at age 11. Years later she got a journalism degree and helped her brother out on a temporary basis—but when he left, she stayed. The store has 60,000 unique items to keep track of, many with names that are a little cryptic to non-experts. Luckily, the store has specialists in plumbing, paints, electrical, garden, cleaning, and hardware.

The store is on the city's list of businesses to call in an emergency. Both of the stores that engendered it—Smith Hardware and Ocean View—were rebuilt in the aftermath of the 1906 quake, so maybe responding to a crisis is in the DNA as well. Jamie says her father Keith's time of trial was the 1989 Loma Prieta quake, when he convinced his contacts at various companies to send necessary items out here to help rebuild.

For her part, Jamie's been tested by COVID. She asked her staff to take fewer hours at first, while Center continued full medical coverage. "Everyone stayed—I was so moved by them backing us, this business, I'm choking up a bit now. Eventually, we topped up their wages, tried

to make them whole." They've had one staffer working there for over 40 years, and several who've been there over 30.

When she speaks of the business's core values, as often as not, her father comes up. "He was the sort of guy who'd read parts catalogs—for fun. People would come in or call with obscure requests. He'd either think of what they required or a work-around. He was like their Google."

Though there's a Lowe's Home Improvement on the outskirts of San Francisco, the big-box stores haven't really invaded the city proper. Most of the neighborhoods featured in this book have their own small hardware stores, many of them quite old. (I once wrote a group profile of these neighborhood hardware stores for the Chronicle.*)*

Founded in 1896, Fredericksen's Hardware & Paint (3029 Fillmore St.) in posh Pacific Heights sells chandelier cleaner and cocktail napkins along with the usual shovels and drills. Begun in the 1920s, Cole Hardware (2254 Polk St.) in Cole Valley has a long line in ladders and artistic windows—for instance, the San Francisco skyline done in duct tape. Roberts Hardware (1629 Haight St.) has been run by the same family from its start in 1931. On the main drag in the Boho Haight, each year store staffers help local clients build huge mobile art pieces for them to take to Burning Man, the art happening in the Nevada Desert.

1943

OLDEST FARMERS' MARKET

ALEMANY FARMERS' MARKET

100 Alemany Blvd.

The world can feel small sometimes at the Alemany Farmers' Market, the oldest in the city and the state. The stalls have raw materials for dishes from all over. Cucumbers come in Japanese, Persian, and Chinese versions. Spinach is named for Malabar, lemons for Lisbon, and eggplant for India. There are stalls staffed by farmers from all over California with broccoli in shades of green, purple, and yellow; mauve carrots; and daikon radishes, milky skins hiding their hot pink-innards. And, when your shopping bags are full and your appetite's high, carts offer steaming Salvadoran pupusas and Chinese bao buns stuffed with pork. Where many farmers' markets feel post-hippie, with the clients and farmers mainly white, this low-cost market features people—and food—of many colors.

These days there are few things less controversial than a farmers' market, but the founders of this one had to fight to get it going. In his memoir, *A Sicilian in America,*

organizer John Brucato says he was called "a radical, a communist, and many other affectionate names" in his decade-long struggle to get it firmly established.

Brucato got the idea during the war years when the canneries closed, the metal needed by the military, and pears harvested in nearby Marin County looked set to rot on the ground. A call went out to San Franciscans through the Victory-Garden network, and thousands of city folk drove to the orchards to buy the fruit. Without the middlemen, farmers could sell at a higher price, and consumers could purchase at a lower one.

But gas was in limited supply back then, so Brucato and others negotiated for the use of a vacant lot next to a mortician's in SOMA, and the market was born—six truckloads sold out in less than two hours. This was (apologies) still small potatoes and didn't much bother the food industry's established players. But when a subsequent market pulled in 135 farmers and 50,000 consumers, a war on many fronts began. The food wholesalers and grocery associations pushed City Hall to stop the gathering, encouraging inspectors to search for rotten produce. But the organizers of what became known as the people's market had public opinion on their side. They soon got the project on a municipal ballot and won a whopping 85 percent of the votes. And so the city found a permanent site for it, albeit one on its southern fringes, one that was soon surrounded by highways.

Where selling at many a farmers' market is a laid-back affair, here samples are offered and a pitch is made. I point at a homely globe covered in fur: "Hairy gourds go well in chicken soup," I'm told. I palpate a lime—something of a no-no, but it's a citrus fruit so I feel okay about it. "The yellow limes are juicier. You can tell, right?" It's a nice thing to come here in the run-up to Thanksgiving to remind yourself—if reminding is needed—of the luck of living in a land of such plenty. Here, it seems, the products of an earthly paradise came and took back that parking lot.

Or you might feel that way, if, in peak harvest season, you're able to find parking. If the market's spirit is one of friendly competition, there's no live and let live in the process of finding a spot for your car.

A three-minute walk from the Farmers' Market is the city's oldest mosque, the Islamic Center of San Francisco (400 Crescent Ave.). A congregation founded in 1959, it occupies a barn-shaped building. "The choice of Crescent Ave, the symbol of Islam, for the location, that was a coincidence," says director Ovays Patel, an operations supervisor at Recology, a creative recycling center.

From the start, the congregation has been multiethnic, with members whose families come from Malaysia, India, Pakistan, Saudi Arabia, Libya, and Sudan. Thursday night dinners have helped to cement ties between people from disparate places with disparate ways of keeping the faith. About 225 people will muster for major holidays like Eid, sometimes parking, with permission, in neighbors' driveways. After the ban on immigration from Muslim-majority countries was passed in 2017, "We Love Muslims" signs popped up all over Bernal Heights. "We have a good relationship," Patel says, "with our neighbors."

1931

OLDEST CONFECTIONARY

SHAW'S CANDY

122 W Portal Ave.

The city's oldest candy shop was founded by Douglas Shaw. Originally named Karamel Corn, this West Portal store offered 35 ice cream flavors, all prepared in house, and 300 varieties of candies, some made here, others brought in. Among the handmade candies, regular customers particularly remember the peanut chocolate clusters, the various fudges, and the rainbow of jelly beans.

Over the years the store accumulated a museum-level collection of Pez dispensers, each generation's obsessions documented in their plastic-head handles. With the help of his brother Jack, an economics graduate of Stanford, Shaw eventually expanded the company to 50 stores. A simple red-and-white logo adorned its stickers, but its interior was psychedelic, a place of many colors over a red-and-white tiled floor. The total effect was something mad, a setting that would suit Gene Wilder's Willy Wonka from the 1971 film *Willy Wonka and the Chocolate Factory.*

"As a child," one longtime patron recently said, "I went in there with my mom after karate class. Later I took my children and then grandchildren there, turning them on to a variety of jelly beans and old-school candies."

The store eventually passed out of the family's hands, and a couple of years ago it almost died altogether. When "For Rent" signs went up, the locals panicked. One of them, a mother who often took her kids there, went into action. Diana Zogaric had no previous background in the field—she'd worked as a film editor, sometimes producing content for the likes of Salesforce. Certainly, she didn't expect the amount of dry-rot she found in the walls during her renovation in August 2020. A savvy marketer, she documented her efforts, pleased that neighbors would sometimes knock on the windows and give her a thumbs-up.

The décor now riffs on the old branding of the place, with the red of Shaw's labels reproduced in certain accent walls and some wild wallpaper at the back. But there have also been some shifts: A motto in pink neon now glows over the ice-cream and fudge counter: "Candy, Ice Cream, Happiness." ("Words to live by," Zogaric says.) And the floor is now checker-boarded in black-and-white.

There's still a decent collection of Pezes for sale: Scooby Doo, Little Mermaid, Hello, Kitty, Princess Leia, Garfield, and Bart Simpson, as well as those retro candies, Pop Rocks. But most of the candy is hand-made, small-batch—cocoa-dusted almonds, malt-chocolate balls, mint nonpareils, and sour strips.

Zogaric has learned what's what with their core offering, fudge. She has figured out, for instance, that the ingredients—butter, cream, and sugar—need to be heated in a big kettle to a temperature near 238 degrees, and then cooled overnight. She and her staff do both regular fudge and penuche (which uses brown sugar). She's learned how to swirl it to give it a fancy patina on top. "You need some muscle when you're mixing the fudge," she recently told a TV reporter who came here to record a short hit.

Zogaric gives her mainly teenage staff some leeway with fudge flavors—after all, they're nearer the average customer's age. But when it came time for her first Easter, she realized she that wanted no input. The Michigan native grew up Catholic, with a no-holds-barred Easter, and insisted the bunnies and carrots should be made of solid milk chocolate, not hollowed out. As for the ice creams, they now come from the Mission's longtime ice-cream maker Mitchell's, and there are sprinkles of all colors and nuts as toppings. Zogaric has a retro cooler on wheels, in Shaw's Red, that she can bring to kids' parties, with several flavors of ice cream and all those toppings.

Shaw's street, West Portal Avenue, has long served as the main shopping drag for a pretty, historic neighborhood near it, St. Francis Wood. Opened in 1912, the development borrowed ideas from the City Beautiful movement popularized at the Chicago World's Fair in 1893. The idea was to combine the convenience of the city and the green space of the country.

Mission accomplished. Many of the pastel, period-revival homes are by leading San Francisco architects—Willis Polk (known for his Hallidie Building); Timothy Pflueger (the Castro Theatre), Bernard Maybeck (the Palace of Fine Arts), and Julia Morgan (Hearst Castle). The utilities are buried here, the houses set back from the street, the sidewalks made of interlocking bricks. At one of the main entries to the neighborhood from an arterial road there's a pair of neoclassical gates, and an elaborate, tiered fountain designed by Henry Gutterson sits near the eastern end of St. Francis Boulevard.

1908

OLDEST PHARMACY

CENTRAL DRUG STORE

4494 Mission St.

The Bay Area has bred some storied drug-store chains over the years—Owl Drugs (1892–1940s) and Long Drugs (1938–2008) to name two. But one small pharmacy in the Excelsior has quietly outlasted these national players. Central Drug Store was started in 1908 on Mission Street just before it exits the city's southern end, and it's still there, with its well-staffed pharmacy counter and stock reminiscent of a general store. In addition to Anacin and aspirin you can get toys, board games, American flags, Russell Stover candies, birthday cards, even ceramic tea-bag holders.

Central's first two owners were of Northern European descent (surnames: Brenner and Stahl), reflecting the demographics of the working-class neighborhood. In the 1910s and '20s, the neighborhood saw more Italian Americans move in, and the DeVecenzi family purchased the store in 1927. William Tonelli soon joined them as a junior partner and bought out the others near the mid-century. Ever since, it's been owed by the Tonellis, with William and his wife Elsie running it until his death in 1991 and their son Jerry taking over after that.

"My mother still comes in, 30 years after my father's death," Tonelli says, "She's 95 now. All the other stock, the non-drugstore stuff—that's her. She pores over catalogs and finds nice things. The tea-bag holders, that's her—she loves tea."

When William met Elsie in the 1940s, he was a pharmacist and she a clerk. "My mother answered a help-wanted ad in 1940. They were married 10 years later." The store has become something of a love shack since then. There's a star on the floor where Tonelli's sister and her soon-to-be husband met, and one of the guys who worked with Tonelli as a stock-boy in high school met the woman who'd become his wife here.

The store stands on the corner of a side street and has a big mural on one outside wall featuring the Grateful Dead's Jerry Garcia. The store has had a few other famous clients: Congresswoman Jackie Speier, Giants pitcher Juan Marichal, and the man who was, for a time, the oldest living New York Yankee, Rugger Ardizoia. Central has been a pillar of this community, a frequent donor to schools and social clubs—as well as to the local Jerry Garcia day celebration (more on this below).

Tonelli has seen a lot change since he started helping out here in the 1970s and then went to pharmacy school at the University of Idaho. Its demographics have shifted towards Americans of Filipino, Chinese, and Mexican descent. The main drag was, he recalls, once full of mom-and-pop shops like Central. "There was Zimmerman stationery, Ferrera Hardware," he says. "And Gordon's clothing, Farrow's department store, a shoe shop, a shoe-repair shop, a paint store. The neighborhood felt like a small town." Those are mainly gone now, replaced with chain stores and auto-repair shops.

"We're tied to the neighborhood," says Tonelli. "They depend on you. They talk to you about important things—things you can't necessarily ask at a Walgreen's." And, indeed, on the day I visit, at the back counter there are two locals asking in-depth questions about their prescriptions, with one of them then recounting, in detail, the back-and-forth with his doctors.

The store had some young staff stocking its shelves, and Tonelli is proud of the store's role as often, the first employer of many local kids. He also likes when he gets to serve and advise several generations of the same family. "We have people who came here with their parents when they were 4 or 5 years old, and now they're coming back with their kids. When they come in, as adults, I see memories in my head."

Local hero Jerry Garcia spent his first five years living near here, just off Mission with his father (121 Amazon Ave.). At the corner of Mission and Amazon is a plaque showing a likeness of the Dead frontman in his Touch-of-Grey period, with this quote: "What we're trying to do is expand rather than narrow."

After his father died, 5-year-old Garcia moved to another home in the neighborhood to live with his grandparents (87 Harrington St.). At that side street's corner is another plaque, this one featuring Garcia in his early years with the Dead. It's etched with the words: "My grandmother listened to country, my mother listened to opera . . . I was in the middle of music."

Each summer in the Excelsior's main green space, the 313-acre John McLaren Park, the amphitheater named for him hosts Garcia Day, a multi-act festival featuring the sort of good-time music he played and enjoyed.

1962

OLDEST COMMUNITY-BASED SUICIDE HOTLINE

SAN FRANCISCO SUICIDE PREVENTION

Location Undisclosed

The first suicide hotline in the nation run outside the confines of a hospital was started by Englishman Bernard Mayes. A Cambridge-educated Anglican priest, he served for a long time as BBC Radio's San Francisco correspondent. The pieces ending with his elegantly voiced sign-off, "This is Bernard Mayes in San Francisco," gave people around the world a sense of the city's character in the heady 1960s.

Rightly or wrongly, Mayes had heard that his adoptive city was a magnet for suicidal people. "I did feel what was really needed was a compassionate ear, someone to talk to," he once told the *Chronicle*. For a time he couldn't find a landlord willing to have this hotline for a tenant, until a man renting out a room in the Tenderloin proved to be a survivor, showing Mayes the scars on both his arms before offering him the space.

For a time, the hotline was just Mayes, with one phone. He put up cardboard ads in the buses: "Thinking of ending it all? Call Bruce . . . SF Suicide Prevention." (The current number is 415-781-0500.)

On his first night he got just one call, but there were 10 by the end of the week. Soon he found others to help answer the phones and, after a decade, the operation firmly established, he bowed out, believing "the people who start things mustn't stay too long." By then he was also working to help set up National Public Radio, as its first chair, and helping to run the San Francisco affiliate, KQED.

The organization has carried on its good, difficult work. From taking 200 calls a month, it now fields as many as 175 a day, about 65,000 calls a year, with six paid staff helping to train an average of 125 community volunteers. Though it's impossible to measure the hotline's impact over time, the *Chronicle* reported that San Francisco's suicide rate declined by almost two-thirds over the hotline's first 50 years. Since its founding, the model has been emulated in 500 cities across the nation, with similar hotlines now in every state.

The volunteers don't read from a script. Instead they're encouraged to find their own personal ways of responding. Van Hedwall, Director of Programs, says: "We give them 40 hours of didactic training, classroom training, and then 30 hours of mentorship, where they sit with a more seasoned counselor. They explore their own reasons for coming to this work, what do they think the work is. We have young people who volunteer, old people, all races, creeds, colors."

The organization also offers a grief group and a group focused on young people at risk. "My heart belongs to the youth of the city," Hedwall says. "I want to make sure they are safe." The group helps train police, firefighters, and 911 operators in how to handle calls from those voicing

Suicide hotline founder Bernard Mayes

suicidal thoughts. In 2019 the group merged with a mental-health organization long established in the Bay Area, the Felton Institute.

As for Mayes, he moved away for a while to teach communications at the University of Virginia, where he became a well-respected faculty member. He also wrote radio and stage plays. At the end of his life he returned to San Francisco, to Bernal Heights, and was honored in 2012 for his role in setting up this service by the Night Ministry. After a long struggle with Parkinson's, he died in 2014.

"I am so proud to be the person stepping into his shoes," Hedwall says. "You could never fill them, but I'm proud to be carrying on the work he started."

"One of the reasons I think Bernie [Mayes] started the helpline was the [Golden Gate] bridge being here. I don't know why exactly but it's always been a magnet," Hedwall says. For years the bridge has had phones attached to it connected to counselors and trained first responders, but still an average of 30 people per year have committed suicide by jumping off the structure—more than 1,800 people since the bridge's completion in 1937. That is about to change, with the installation of a steel net just below the bridge's walkway—at a cost of $215 million.

Denis Mulligan, manager at the Golden Gate Bridge, Highway and Transportation District, recently told the Los Angeles Times*: "Construction is expensive, but to be able to save 30 lives per year . . . it's 30 families, 30 groups of friends that won't be left adrift struggling with the loss of people who they love."*

Bibliography

Herbert Asbury, *The Barbary Coast* (Alfred A. Knopf, 1933)

Bob Barde, with Pat Cunneen, *South End: Sport and Community at the Dock of the Bay* (Gibbons Press, 2019)

Robert W. Bowen, *San Francisco's Presidio* (Arcadia Publishing, 2005)

Herb Caen, *The Best of Herb Caen, 1960–1975* (Chronicle Books, 1991)

Herb Caen, *Don't Call it Frisco* (Doubleday & Co., Inc., 1953)

Herb Caen, *Herb Caen's New Guide to San Francisco* (Doubleday & Co., Inc., 1957)

Ruth Wertzberger Carlson, *Secret San Francisco: A Guide to the Weird, Wonderful, and Obscure* (Reedy Press, 2019)

Philip P. Choy, *San Francisco Chinatown: A Guide to its History & Architecture* (City Lights, 2012)

Denise E. Clifton, *Tables from the Rubble* (Tandemvines Media, 2017)

Ronald Fimrite, *Winged O: The Olympic Club of San Francisco, 1860–2009* (Olympic Club, 2010)

Katherine Girlich, *San Francisco Zoo* (Arcadia Publishing, 2009)

Richard Harned, *The Palace Hotel* (Arcadia Publishing, 2009)

Edith Heath, *Philosophies* (Berkeley Design Books, 2020)

Anne Evers Hitz, *Lost Department Stores of San Francisco* (History Press, 2020)

Cleve Jones, *When We Rise: My Life in the Movement* (Hachette Books, 2016)

Gary Kamiya, *Cool Gray City of Love: 49 Views of San Francisco* (Bloomsbury, 2013)

Gary Kamiya and Paul Madonna, *Spirits of San Francisco: Voyages Through the Unknown City* (Bloomsbury, 2020)

Kathleen Manning and Jim Dickson, *San Francisco's Ocean Beach* (Arcadia Publishing, 2003)

Malcolm Margolin, *The Ohlone Way: Indian Life in the San Francisco-Monterey Bay Area* (Heyday, 1978)

John A. Martini, *Sutro's Glass Palace: The Story of the Sutro Baths* (Hole in the Head Press, 2014)

Frances Moffat, *Dancing on the Brink of the World: The Rise and Fall of San Francisco Society* (G.P. Putnam's Sons, 1977)

Elizabeth Pepin and Lewis Watts, *Harlem of the West: The San Francisco Fillmore Jazz Era* (Chronicle Books, 2006)

Christopher Pollock, *San Francisco's Golden Gate Park: A Thousand and Seventeen Acres of Stories* (Norfolk Press, 2020)

Janet Lynn Roseman, et al., *Gump's Since 1861* (Sue Katz & Associates, 1991)

Fred Rosenbaum, *Visions of Reform: Congregation Emanu-El and the Jews of San Francisco, 1849–1999* (Judah L. Magnus Museum, 2000)

Frances Bransten Rothmann, *The Haas Sisters of Franklin Street* (Heyday, 1979)

David Talbot, *Season of the Witch* (Free Press, 2012)

Bonnie Tsui, *American Chinatown: A People's History of Five Neighborhoods* (Free Press, 2009)

Gregory L. Wellman, *A History of Alcatraz Island, 1853–2008* (Arcadia Publishing, 2008)

Judy Yung et al., *San Francisco's Chinatown* (Arcadia Publishing, 2016)

Alan Ziajka and Robert Elias, *University of San Francisco* (Arcadia Publishing, 2015)

INDEX